P

PROFILE BOOKS

25 YEARS OF **NOVARTIS**
250 YEARS OF INNOVATION

ᨸ NOVARTIS

1758 Johann Rudolf Geigy-Gemuseus founds the trading company J.R. Geigy.

1859 Silk dyestuff manufacturer Alexandre Clavel is the first in Switzerland to start producing synthetic dyestuffs.

>> 1860 Geigy company officer Johann Jakob Müller-Pack also starts production of synthetic dyestuffs.

1861

1862

1863

1864 Gerber & Uhlmann dyestuff factory set up in Basel.

1865

1866

1867

1868

1869

>> 1870

1871 Durand & Huguenin dyestuff factory set up in Basel.

1872

1873 Clavel sells his factory to Robert Bindschedler and Albert Busch.

1874

1875

1876

1877

1878

1879

>> 1880

1881 Durand & Huguenin founds the first Swiss chemicals factory abroad in Saint-Fons (France).

1882

1183

1884 Bindschedler & Busch is renamed Gesellschaft für Chemische Industrie in Basel (later CIBA).

1885

1886 Alfred Kern and Edouard-Constant Sandoz found the chemical company Kern & Sandoz.

1887

1888

1889

>> 1890

1891

1892

1893 Robert Bindschedler founds Basler Chemische Fabrik AG.

1894

1895

1896

1897

1898 Gesellschaft für Chemische Industrie in Basel acquires the neighboring factory Anilinfarbenwerk, formerly A. Gerber & Cie.

1899

>> 1900

1901

1902

1903

Geigy

CIBA

Sandoz

Novartis

1907

1908 — Gesellschaft für Chemische Industrie in Basel acquires Basler Chemische Fabrik AG.

1909

1910

1911

1996 — Sandoz and Ciba surprise everyone on March 7 by announcing their merger to form Novartis.
The Swiss Novartis companies appear in the Commercial Register on December 20.

1997 — The chemicals business of Ciba-Geigy is spun off to form an independent company under the name Ciba Specialty Chemicals, Basel.

1998 — The Novartis Institute for Functional Genomics is founded in La Jolla (California, USA).

1999

2000 — Novartis is one of the first companies to sign the UN Global Compact.
Novartis merges its agricultural business with that of AstraZeneca: the result is Syngenta, a company focusing entirely on agriculture.

2001 — *Gleevec*/*Glivec* receives marketing authorization for the US and European markets.
It is used to treat chronic myeloid leukemia, a form of blood cancer.

2002 — The antimalaria drug *Coartem* is included in the World Health Organization's list of essential medicines.
Novartis reorganizes its worldwide research network, founding the Novartis Institutes for BioMedical Research, Cambridge (Massachusetts, USA).
Novartis announces its Campus Project: the St. Johann site in Basel is to be completely redesigned.
Novartis acquires the Slovenian generics company Lek, Ljubljana (Slovenia).

2003 — Novartis unites its generics business under the single global brand name of Sandoz.

2004 — The Novartis Institute for Tropical Diseases opens in Singapore.

2005 — Novartis acquires two leading generics manufacturers: the German company Hexal AG, Holzkirchen (Upper Bavaria), and the US company Eon Labs, Inc., New York.

2006 — Novartis diversifies into the vaccines and diagnostics business by acquiring US biotech company Chiron Corporation, Emeryville (California, USA).

2007 — Novartis sells its Medical Nutrition and Gerber business units to concentrate wholly on healthcare.
Novartis opens the Novartis Vaccines Institute for Global Health in Siena (Italy).

2008

2009

2010 — Novartis acquires majority ownership, and concludes an agreement to become the 100 % owner of Alcon, Inc., based in Fort Worth (Texas, USA), and becomes the world leader in eye care.

2011 — Acquisition of Alcon completed. Novartis creates the new Alcon Division, focused on eye care, from Alcon, Inc., CIBA Vision and Novartis Pharmaceuticals Ophthalmics.

2012 — The European Commission grants marketing authorization for the cancer medicine *Afinitor* to treat the most common form of advanced breast cancer.

2013

2014 — Novartis introduces radical restructuring and a new direction for the Company. In a multi-level process, Novartis transforms itself from a broadly based health company to a focused drug company.
Cosentyx is registered in Japan to treat psoriasis and psoriatic arthritis.

2015 — Novartis takes over GSK's oncology products and sells its vaccine and animal health businesses.
Entresto is registered in the USA and the European Union to treat heart failure.

2016

2017 — *Kymriah* is registered in the USA to treat children and young adults with acute lymphoblastic leukemia.

2018 — Novartis sells its involvement in the Consumer Health Joint Venture with GSK.
Novartis acquires the gene therapy specialist AveXis as well as the radiopharmaceutical companies Advanced Accelerator Applications and Endocyte.

2019 — The eyecare division (Alcon) is spun off and listed on the stock exchange as an independent company.
Zolgensma is registered in the USA to treat spinal muscular atrophy in children under two years of age.

2020 — Novartis takes over the biotechnology firm The Medicines Company.

25 Years of Novartis.
250 Years of Innovation.

Foreword Joerg Reinhardt
Conception and text Walter Dettwiler
Contributions Carole Billod, Philipp Gafner, Daniela Hoegger

Contents

Joerg Reinhardt
Chairman of the Board of Directors

Dear Reader,

The merger of Ciba-Geigy and Sandoz 25 years ago was a milestone in the long and successful history of Swiss industry. Because of its size, complexity and strategic direction, it also set new benchmarks internationally.

What hardly anyone considered possible at the beginning of 1996 – the amalgamation of two traditional, medium-sized Basel companies with distinct identities and cultures – became reality and triggered a chain reaction that led to new contours for the pharmaceutical industry and fresh impulses for Switzerland and the City of Basel.

At a stroke, one of the largest pharmaceutical companies in the world emerged from two companies chiefly active in the chemical industry. It set itself up as a global player and made scientific innovation its focus.

The merger was both a cesura and a continuum. At the press conference of March 7, 1996, recalling the successful industrial tradition of Sandoz and Ciba-Geigy and understanding the need for constant further development, Chairman of the Board Alex Krauer formulated the reason for the merger with these words: "To be good in times of rapid change is not enough. Only the best will make it. Novartis is the expression of this will."

The goal of belonging to the leading companies of the world has shaped Novartis since its foundation a quarter of a century ago. It can be felt today just as strongly as it could then. The proactive and courageous attitude led again and again to portfolio adjustments. But these changes were constantly driven by the recognition that success also depends on how far the company dares to invest in innovative and strongly growing fields of activity.

Against this background, after the merger Novartis took leave of Ciba's classical chemicals activities and later of its agribusiness, which led to the foundation of Syngenta. It concentrated on its already well developed pharmaceutical activities, which we have continuously built up in the past 25 years. In this, we were always prepared to employ the latest technologies: our aspiration was always not only to exist in global competition, but to take a leading position.

Part of these efforts, which began over 20 years ago, was the establishment of a global research network through the foundation of the Novartis Institutes for BioMedical Research and other institutes. Today, our research and development activities include a total of around 20,000 scientists, doctors and health specialists who work closely with internationally leading universities, research institutions and hospitals.

Innovation is deeply embedded in our DNA. Whereas in 1996, Novartis invested around 2 billion US dollars in research and development, today it is around 9 billion US dollars a year. The willingness to take entrepreneurial risks and pour substantial resources into medical areas previously scarcely researched is an important element of our strategy and also forms the foundation stone of our success.

Being prepared to take risks was already a hallmark of our predecessor companies. Around half a century ago, they achieved important medical milestones in transplantation medicine and neurology, to highlight two areas. Building on these successes and driven by the resolve to tread new pathways, in the last 25 years we have been able to attain significant progress in, for example, oncology, the treatment of cardiovascular illnesses and the field of infectious diseases. Thereby we have made a contribution towards broadening the spectrum of medical therapy approaches.

Today, we are penetrating new therapeutical areas like gene technology or nuclear medicine, and are among the foremost in accelerating our research efforts through the deployment of artificial intelligence. Just like a quarter of a century ago, we strive to be one of the best in order to fulfill our mission: to help millions of people worldwide to lead longer and healthier lives.

Novartis' roots stretch much further back than the merger. However, the driving forces of the company have always been the same. They are shaped by the desire to push medical innovation forward in the interests of humanity and to make a contribution to social development, prosperity and progress – whether in Basel, in Switzerland or elsewhere in the world. That will remain so in the future.

1 READY FOR LIFT-OFF

THE FOUNDING OF BASEL'S DYE FACTORIES 1859–1908

Europe first shone in artificial night-light 200 years ago. Instead of candles, gas now lit the houses of the well-off. Gas lights soon lit up the streets of the towns as well. The gas was obtained from coal, which produced large quantities of unpleasant, smelly tar as waste: this was tipped into rivers, resulting in severe environmental pollution. In 1833, the German chemist Friedlieb Ferdinand Runge investigated the possible uses of tar. In it, he found aniline. This had already been discovered in 1826. In 1856, the English chemistry student William Henry Perkin conducted experiments with this colorless, oily liquid. He was hoping to produce synthetic quinine, for this efficacious antimalarial agent was very much in demand in the British colonies. Instead of white quinine, Perkin obtained an almost black product, from which he isolated a substance that dyed silk a violet color. He named it mauveine, after the French for mallow blossom. Perkin had his invention patented and founded a production site close to London with support from his family. But mauveine did not remain the only synthetic dye for long. In 1858, the French chemist Emanuel Verguin discovered aniline red. He sold his process to the silk dyeworks of Renard frères et Franc in Lyon (France). They patented the new dye, named fuchsine after the red blooms of the fuchsia, and started production. Fuchsine was easier to manufacture than mauveine and it was more productive and versatile. The product triggered a veritable gold rush: dyers and dye merchants, manufacturers and chemists tried to discover similar substances or at least to acquire formulations. Compared with the natural vegetable, animal or mineral-based dyes used since ancient times, these synthetic dyestuffs allowed greater fastness, lower costs and also the possibility of producing textiles in every conceivable shade of color.

CIBA Just three years after the discovery of mauveine, aniline dyes were being produced in Basel. In 1840, Alexandre Clavel (1805–1873) from Lyon had taken over a silk dyeworks in Lesser Basel. Thanks to family connections with Renard frères et Franc he was able to acquire the license for the fuchsine process. He immediately began to produce dyes in a laboratory close to the dyeworks. Due to increasing complaints from the population about the pollutant emissions, production was forbidden in 1863. The operation had to be moved outside the city. Clavel built his new factory in what was then a rural district on Klybeckstrasse alongside the Rhine. In 1873, he sold this to the chemist Robert Bindschedler (1844–1901) and the businessman Albert Busch (1836–1884). The new owners quickly expanded the company: within a year the workforce of about 30 people had more than doubled. In 1884, Bindschedler & Busch became a modern corporation. It now called itself Gesellschaft für Chemische Industrie in Basel. The abbreviated form CIBA, which was initially used only for products, became the official company name in 1945.

Basler Chemische Fabrik In 1892, Robert Bindschedler left CIBA, which he had first run as a Director from 1884–1889 and subsequently helped to shape as a member of the Board of Directors. In 1893, he founded Basler Chemische Fabrik (BCF) in Kleinhüningen, also on the Lesser Basel side of the Rhine. This company became a listed stock corporation in 1898 with capital of 1.5 million Swiss francs. Six years later, BCF acquired an additional production facility in Monthey (Canton of Valais, Switzerland). In 1908, the Board of Directors of BCF began to consider a merger with CIBA. Initial negotiations began in June, and just six weeks later representatives of both companies signed the merger agreement. According to this agreement, BCF merged retrospectively into CIBA from July 1, 1908. In November of the same year the General Meeting of BCF approved the merger. For every five BCF shares held, the shareholders received three CIBA shares. To finance the takeover, CIBA had to increase its share capital by 3.5 million Swiss francs. With the merger, the patents held by BCF were transferred to CIBA.

J.R.Geigy The trading company J.R.Geigy was founded in 1758. It traded raw materials used in the manufacture of dyestuffs or medicinal products. In the 1830s the company started to manufacture natural dyes itself, initially on an artisanal, then from 1859 on an industrial basis. In Lesser Basel, Johann Rudolf Geigy-Merian (1830–1917) built a so-called extract factory with a steam boiler and production plant where dyewood was milled and ground to extract the dyestuffs. In 1860, Geigy-Merian handed the extract factory over to the authorized signatory of Geigy, Johann Jakob Müller-Pack (1825–1899), who had founded his own company, J.J. Müller & Cie., in the same year. Immediately after the takeover, Müller-Pack expanded the small plant and began to produce synthetic dyes. In 1862 he bought a plot of land on Rosentalmatten to build a second factory there. At the Great London Exposition of 1862, the dyes of J.J. Müller & Cie. proved a sensation. But the meteoric rise of the company came to an abrupt end: in 1864 J.J. Müller & Cie. lost a lawsuit over the contamination of groundwater and was forced into bankruptcy. Geigy-Merian bought back the business, including the extract factory and the aniline production. In 1901 it became a corporation. Most of the stock stayed in the hands of the Geigy family, however.

Gerber & Uhlmann A few months after fuchsine was patented by Verguin, the Alsatian Jean Gerber-Keller (1809–1884) and his son Armand Gerber (1837–1886) discovered a new red dye. They called it azalein. Gerber-Keller wanted to have it patented. The French patent law of 1844 protected the end product, but not the process. Since azalein was similar to the fuchsine of Renard frères et Franc in color, Gerber lost a court case brought by the Lyon manufacturers. In 1862, the two Gerbers came to Switzerland and joined the dyeworks of Gaspard Dollfus (1812–1889) as chemists. In 1864,

Armand Gerber set up in business himself, founding Gerber & Uhlmann on Klybeckstrasse together with a businessman named Uhlmann. The company was bought by CIBA in 1898.

Durand & Huguenin Louis Durand (1837–1901) was chief chemist with Société de la Fuchsine in Lyon prior to emigrating to Basel. From 1866 to 1870 he worked in Clavel's dye factory. In 1871 he took over a chemical factory in the north-west of the city. This had been founded by Gaspard Dollfus, the builder and leaseholder of the Basel gasworks, in 1860. From 1872 Durand's brother-in-law, Daniel Edouard Huguenin (1845–1899), also held a stake in the company.

Sandoz Alfred Kern (1850–1893), an extremely successful chemist, left CIBA at the end of 1884 due to differences of opinion on the use of his patents. Kern met with the wealthy businessman Edouard-Constant Sandoz (1853–1928) who, as authorized signatory for Durand & Huguenin, was prohibited from holding the interest he wanted in the company. The two of them founded Chemische Fabrik Kern & Sandoz as a general partnership in 1886. Like other dye factories, the new company was located outside the residential area of the time, on about 11,000 square meters of land right next to Durand & Huguenin and the municipal gasworks. In 1895, the company was changed to a corporation called Chemische Fabrik vormals Sandoz. From 1939 it was called Sandoz AG.

Why in Basel? At the end of the 19th century, there were six dye factories in Basel – an extraordinary concentration! Various factors had contributed to the attractiveness of the city at different times. A crucial reason why the chemical industry settled in Basel was its position at the hub of the important textile center of the Upper Rhine. The Basel silk ribbon weaving industry and the numerous textile factories and textile printing works in Alsace and South Baden needed large quantities of dyes. The first chemical companies obtained their know-how from France. French patent law, which was not favorable to chemists, prompted many of them to seek their fortune in Basel. Another important factor for the location was the Rhine: it provided the water that was needed for manufacture, and at the same time production waste could be easily disposed of in the river. A further advantage was the very good transport links offered by the city: the location on the elbow of the Rhine and its position on the border favored early connection with the sea and the international railroad network as well as the rapid development of transportation systems. Trains had been running daily from Basel to France and Germany since 1853. Furthermore, due to the high density of chemical and pharmaceutical companies in Basel, there was a vibrant culture of personnel exchange accompanied by an equally lively transfer of knowledge and information. And finally, the close proximity of competitors facilitated innovation.

Geigy Basel. Schoren residential colony
with the Bitterli family. 1890s.

Sandoz Basel. Workers' children
in front of spirit building. Around 1902.

001
Alexandre Clavel (1805 – 1873). Around 1860.
Alexandre Clavel from Lyon settled in Basel
in 1838, and in 1840 took over a silk dyeworks on Rebgasse. The marriage of his step-
daughter Rosine Henriette Oswald to silk
dyestuff manufacturer Joseph Renard
from Lyon provided Clavel with invaluable
knowledge: he learned how to manufacture
fuchsine (aniline red). From 1859, he became the first person in Switzerland to produce synthetic dyestuffs in his laboratory.
How-ever, Clavel's activities slowed down
due to complaints about the pollution from
his works; in 1863, the government of Basel
prohibited the production of aniline red
and imposed constraints on the manufacture
of other dyestuffs. In response to this, in
1864 Clavel moved his dyestuff production
outside the city to Klybeckstrasse on the
Rhine. In 1873, he sold his factory to R. Bindschedler and A. Busch.

002
**Management and chemists from the Bind-
schedler & Busch chemical factory.
Early 1880s.**
Robert Bindschedler (1844 – 1901) – group
photo: middle row, eighth from left – grew up
with his five siblings in Winterthur (north-
eastern Switzerland). After completing high
school, he studied chemistry at the Federal
Polytechnic Institute in Zurich. From 1865,
he worked as a chemist, including at Geigy.
In 1871, he joined A. Clavel's aniline dyestuffs
factory, which he went on to acquire together
with businessman Albert Busch in 1873.
In 1884, Bindschedler & Busch became the
Gesellschaft für Chemische Industrie in
Basel (which later became CIBA), and Bindschedler was Director until 1889. In 1893,
Bindschedler founded his own factory, which
he expanded to form Basler Chemische
Fabrik Bindschedler and later Basler
Chemische Fabrik AG. The company merged
with the Gesellschaft für Chemische
Industrie in Basel in 1908. Bindschedler was
awarded an honorary doctorate by the
University of Zurich in recognition of his
contribution to the chemical industry
in Basel. He was convicted of fraud in 1900
after he had breached a contract with
German company Hoechst governing sales of
Antipyrine, and died the following year in
prison.

001

002

CIBA Basel. Staff of the dyeworks.
1893.

CIBA Basel. Staff of manufacturing sites 38 and 39. 1893.

CIBA Basel. Laboratory staff.
1893.

CIBA Basel. Staff of the Sched-E.
manufacturing site. 1893.

003
**Oil painting of the Geigy-Gemuseus family.
1782.**
The Basel economy was dominated by
silk ribbon weaving from the 17th to the early
20th century. In addition, there were a
number of hosiery and textile factories.
The second half of the 18th century also saw
developments in Indienne manufacturing
(hand-painted, later industrially printed
cotton fabric). Dyers and textile printers
needed chemicals for their work, which
allowed trade in "dyers' drugs" to flourish
alongside the textile industry. Several
so-called drug or material goods companies
of this type emerged in Basel in the 18th
century. As well as stocking up with acids
and bases, dyers and printers increasingly
employed ready-to-use dyestuff powders.
In 1758, businessman Johann Rudolf Geigy-
Gemuseus (1733–1793) opened a drug trading
business: he imported and distributed dried
plant-, animal- and mineral-based raw
materials, which were used for manufacturing
medications and dyestuffs.

004
**Bindschedler & Busch company premises.
1879.**

003

004

Geigy Basel. Management,
office workers and chemists
in front of the Bäumlihof,
the Geigy family's villa in Basel.
1888.

Heinrich Mohn-Imobersteg's CIBA
agency in Moscow (Russia). 1897.

005
Johann Jakob Müller-Pack (1825–1899).
Around 1862.

Johann Jakob Müller-Pack completed a
commercial apprenticeship in Basel.
In 1856, he was appointed authorized signatory for J.R. Geigy & Heusler and in 1858
he took over management of Geigy's extract
dyestuff factory. Two years later, Müller-
Pack acquired the company and began
producing synthetic dyestuffs. When a family
in the neighborhood suffered symptoms
of poisoning, he was sentenced to a fine and
high pension and compensation payments.
The authorities also decided to install pipes
leading to the Rhine and charge the costs
to his company. Müller-Pack left Basel at the
end of 1864 and moved to Paris. There
he tried to exploit or sell his patents and processes in an aniline factory in order to
pay his debts in Basel. He entrusted all his
factories to J.R. Geigy-Merian, who purchased them by auction in 1868. Müller-Pack
was unsuccessful in Paris so he returned
to Basel. He tried to set up a new company
together with a businessman friend, but
it soon went bankrupt. In 1870, Müller-Pack
opened a business for dyestuffs and the
production of technical items in Basel.

006
Prints of aniline blue from a manufacturing
inspection register of J.J. Müller & Cie. 1862.
The prints on wool muslin show various
shades of the aniline blue produced by
J.J. Müller & Cie. They can be found in an
inspection register which is among the
oldest of its kind in the world.

005

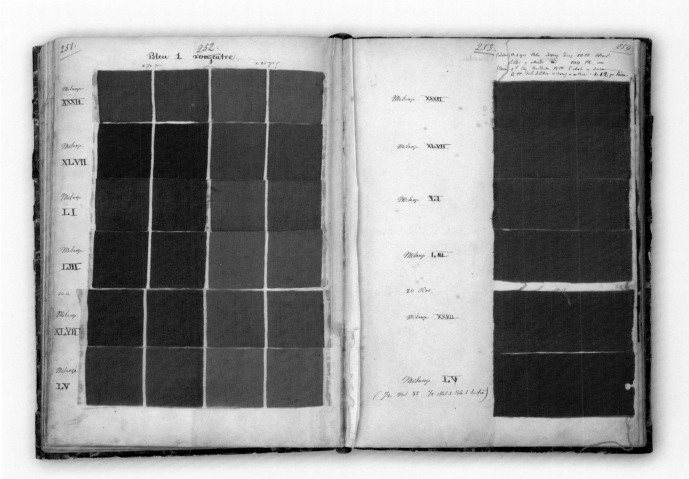

Geigy Basel. Staff of the extract
factory. April 1896.

CIBA Basel. Dr. Goedecke's
medical department. July 27, 1906.

Geigy Basel. Chemist.
Around 1909.

007
**J.R. Geigy factory buildings at Rosental-
matten. Around 1870.**

008
Louis Durand (1837–1901). Around 1900.
Frenchman Louis Durand was head chemist
at Société de la Fuchsine in Lyon before
emigrating to Basel in 1866. From 1866 to
1870, he worked in A. Clavel's silk dyeworks
and aniline dye factory before joining
F. Petersen & Sichler at Schweizerhalle near
Basel. From 1871, he produced his own
synthetic dyestuffs in the former chemical
factory of G. Dollfus in Basel but was forced
to cease production because he did not
have a license. After being granted a license
in 1872, he expanded the factory together
with his brother-in-law Daniel Edouard
Huguenin to form Durand & Huguenin.
Durand withdrew from the business in 1899.

009
Alfred Kern (1850–1893). Around 1890.
Alfred Kern came from one of the oldest
families in the Swiss town of Bülach near
Zurich. Between 1868 and 1870, he studied
chemistry at the Federal Polytechnic Institute
in Zurich before becoming an assistant
there to Johannes Wislicenus. In 1874, Kern
completed a doctorate at the University of
Giessen (Germany). From 1872 through 1878,
he worked at the Chemische Fabrik Karl
Oehler in Offenbach (Germany) and from
1879 to 1884, he was head of the department
for triphenylmethane dyestuffs at Bindschedler & Busch in Basel. In the early 1880s,
Kern came up with several valuable inventions in the field of technical chemistry. His
process for industrial production of phos-
gene and its use in the synthesis of dyestuffs
provided a lasting boost to the color chemistry industry. In 1886, he founded the chemical
company Kern & Sandoz in Basel together
with Edouard-Constant Sandoz. Thanks to
Kern's dyestuff developments, the company
soon enjoyed success.

007

008

009

Sandoz Basel. Chemists Emil
Walder (left) and Oskar Knecht
during a meal break. July 12, 1910.

Geigy Basel. Fitter Kaspar Voegeli.
1913.

010

**Edouard-Constant Sandoz (1853–1928).
Around 1915.**

Edouard-Constant Sandoz began a commercial apprenticeship at a raw silk business
in Basel in 1872. In 1878, he transferred to the
aniline dyestuff factory Etablissements
A. Poirier et G. Dalsace in Saint-Denis near
Paris, before returning to Basel in 1880 and
joining the dyestuff factory Durand & Huguenin. In 1885, he acted as intermediary in
the negotiations between Durand & Huguenin
and the chemist Alfred Kern. The aim of
these negotiations was to set up a new dyestuff factory together. When the negotiations
failed, Sandoz and Kern decided to found
their own company. Kern donated his
manufacturing processes to the new company
as "start-up capital" along with 100,000
Swiss francs, while Sandoz contributed
300,000 Swiss francs. After Kern's sudden
death, Sandoz ran the company on his own.
In 1895, he converted his company into
a stock corporation, taking up the office of
Chairman of the Board, but standing down
after just three months for health reasons.
In 1907, he left the Board of Directors entirely
because he could no longer support the
company's business policies. As majority
shareholder, however, he continued to
influence the management of the company.
He returned to the Board of Directors
in 1916 and began advising the company on
banking and stock exchange issues. In 1921,
Sandoz gave up his mandate for good.

011

First Kern & Sandoz factory. Around 1896.
In the summer of 1885, Alfred Kern applied to
the Basel government for permission to
build a factory. The application was approved
in September, with construction beginning
later that year and being completed by the
spring of 1886. The factory consisted of one
office building with an attached laboratory,
three linked production sheds and a
boiler building housing a steam engine with a
capacity of 12 horsepower.

010

011

THE GOLDEN AGE OF DYESTUFF LABELS

Exchange between East and West

Between 1870 and 1900, Geigy, CIBA and Sandoz dyestuffs became established on the Asian market. They lit up the shops of Vadgadi, Bombay (now Mumbai, India) and Armenian Street in Calcutta (now Kolkata, India), and the bazaars of Shanghai (China) and Kobe (Japan). The Basel companies sent their products to intermediaries and importers. Until the end of the 1930s, the dyestuff packets flooding into Asia were decorated with beautiful chromolithographs. This was the golden age of chromolithography in Europe; it spawned the mass distribution of commercial art as labels for consumer goods.

The chromolithographs from Basel are interesting for two reasons: on the one hand, they illustrate the beginnings of a kind of advertising which was specifically targeted at the individual markets of the world. Carefully crafted and costly to produce, they exercised a seductive effect on the new customer groups to whom they were introducing the dyestuffs of the Basel manufacturers. On the other hand, they were the precursors of trademarks and were legally protected. Contracts between manufacturers and importers regulated their use and distribution from early on. These "trademark labels", as they were called at the time, were often subject to negotiation. The importers took care in selecting the pictures and demanded exclusive rights to them. In return, they committed themselves to taking certain quantities of products from the manufacturers. Because they represented the combined interests of producers and importers against the competition, the dyestuff labels played an essential part in the economic process. As early as the 1880s, dyestuffs came on to the Asian markets in complete packaging, consisting of a main label, a spine label and a suitable seal-like closure – all carefully bonded to a glossy paper envelope that often showed the color of the product inside.

A travel report from 1885 stressed that the Chinese attached less importance to the purity of the dyestuffs than to the careful crafting of the labels. The same appears to have been true in other parts of Asia. With this in mind, the Basel companies faced the fundamental issue about the psychological dimension of images and their emotional influence on the act of buying: they had to speak the client's visual language. To guarantee a product's success, the label had to be attractive, even if that meant raising the price. CIBA, Geigy and Sandoz brought in excellent lithographers to make the dyestuff labels, and they created works of art that reflected the tastes and culture of an international clientele. Unfortunately, the names of most of the original creators are unknown. Only the studios which employed them can be traced – in Paris, in Winterthur and Aarau in Switzerland, and above all in Basel.

Towards 1880, pictures with a commercial character were already part of everyday life. Serving the major brands of the day, they enhanced a product's value, as was the case with Nestlé and Liebig. But the dyestuff labels were not designed as advertising media to set the scene for a product. Far more, they communicated entirely autonomously, independently of

1
Geigy label for Hong Kong. Around 1878.
François Appel printing company, Paris.
Standard labels: the name "Geigy"
and the name of the dyestuff were added
later. Appel worked for the major firms
in Europe from 1875 to 1890.

2
Geigy label for India. 1889.
Printers unknown.
Roman chariot. The medals on the
left represent the prizes that Geigy won
at international exhibitions.

3
Geigy label for Japan. Around 1893.
Lithography: Müller & Trüb printing
company, Aarau (Switzerland).
Two Japanese women in kimonos.
This image is strongly European in style.
These labels were not cheap – in 1893,
1,000 labels cost 37.50 Swiss francs.

4
Geigy label for Japan. Around 1893.
Lithography: Müller & Trüb printing
company, Aarau. Wrestling ring with sumo
wrestler dressed in a ceremonial robe.
The style is very European.

1

2

3

4

5
Label by Bindschedler & Busch (later CIBA)
for India. 1873–1884.
Printers unknown. Probably the Maharaja
Ranbir Singh (1830–1885). The medals again
represent prizes won at major exhibitions.

6
Geigy label for India. 1900s.
Lithography: Gebrüder Lips printing com-
pany, Basel. View of the Babulnath temple in
Bombay (now Mumbai, India) dedicated
to the Hindu god Shiva.

7
Sandoz label for China. Around 1930.
Printers unknown. A cockerel and a hen.

8
Sandoz label for China. Around 1930.
Printers unknown. Five boys riding fish.

9
Closure seal on Geigy dyestuff packaging
for Japan. Around 1893.
The circular seal belongs to the label with
two Japanese women in kimonos (see photo
3, previous page), but is far smaller and
less carefully crafted.

the product. For their pictorial world was aligned to the clientele's cultural environment. To begin with, the dyestuff labels around 1880 manifested a European or partly oriental character. From 1900 the labels systematically took up cultural themes which appealed to the importing countries: local personalities and buildings for India, indigenous flowers and legends for China, women in kimonos for the Japanese Islands. The lithographers drew their inspiration from the Far East, as had the Impressionists before them – especially from Japanese art. In the wake of the flood of Japanese graphics that inundated Europe in the second half of the 19th century, CIBA, Sandoz and Geigy introduced Japanese-style pictures to the markets of Osaka or Yokohama (Japan) – pictures which, however, had been reinterpreted from a European perspective. The images of flowers and birds destined for Shanghai reveal both knowledge of Chinese painting and a distinctly European formal language. From the end of the 19th century onward, Sandoz, CIBA and Geigy contributed to an important economic and cultural exchange by building a bridge between primarily Swiss artists and Asian customers, selling thousands of Swiss lithographs as labels in Delhi and Amritsar (India) and Hong Kong.

The golden age of the magnificent labels circulated by Sandoz, Geigy and CIBA came to an end before the Second World War. Production and administration costs combined with a shift in tastes led to styles that were more in keeping with the objectivity of the new age.

5

6

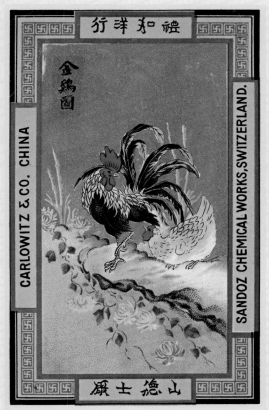

7

8

9

2 EXPORT AND EXPANSION

INTERNATIONAL AND INNOVATIVE FROM THE OUTSET
1881–1914

The aniline dyes manufactured in Basel were exported from the very beginning, initially to France, and then later to the UK and Germany too. In addition to European customers, North American and Asian customers bought dyes from Basel from the 1870s. To begin with, distribution was undertaken by independent trading companies, but was increasingly taken over by subsidiaries as time went on. Basel's chemical companies operated foreign production sites and regional offices from a surprisingly early stage. What initially prompted them to invest abroad? First of all, eagerness to expand or ensure future growth in every case. The protectionist policies of the French and Russian governments also played a significant role in the establishment of factories in those countries. However, there was another motive behind the direct investment of CIBA in the UK: the company was aiming to secure its own supply of products needed for manufacturing.

The first factories in France... In 1881, Durand & Huguenin founded the first Swiss dye factory abroad at Saint-Fons, within the sales area of the textile center of Lyon. Fifteen years after it began operations, three chemists and 85 production and office workers were employed at the 14,500 square meter site. The factory primarily produced fuchsine. When its two founders, Durand and Huguenin, retired from the business, the company began looking for a buyer for the Saint-Fons factory. This decision was not one against manufacturing abroad in general, but against the specific burdens created by the remote site. CIBA acquired the plant in 1900. Geigy had decided as far back as 1891 to set up a French production site. One year later, the company rented a vacant factory building in Maromme, close to the textile center of Rouen. In 1894, it purchased the building. It was a very modest production plant: up until the outbreak of the First World War, it employed only five to seven people manufacturing dyewood extracts.

...and in Germany It was again Durand & Huguenin who established a factory in the Alsatian town of Hüningen, on the border with Switzerland, in 1886. Following the Franco-Prussian War of 1870–1871, large parts of Alsace were annexed by Germany. The journey between the Hüningen production site and the company headquarters was extremely short. Ten years later, the 4,300 square meter site employed one chemist and 15 production workers. Geigy purchased a plot in nearby Grenzach in 1897 and built the first production, office and machinery buildings there over the following two years. Production began at the end of 1898. There were numerous reasons for this investment: first, the facilities at Rosental were outdated. Secondly, the site was becoming increasingly boxed in by residential streets, and residents were being disturbed by noise and odors. Thirdly, the Grenzach site was connected to the German railroad network. The foreign location of this production facility had little significance until the outbreak of the First World War. Before that, the borders in the Basel region were permeable, meaning labor and capital could circulate freely. Grenzach considered itself a suburb of Basel, like the Swiss towns of Muttenz and Birsfelden.

Locations in Russia In 1890, Geigy rented a site with production buildings in Karavayevka, close to Moscow, and began to manufacture dyewood extracts there. The company also sold aniline dyes from Basel through this subsidiary. Geigy later entered into a partnership with a chemical factory in Liepāja (now in Latvia), which prompted Geigy to give up its previous location in 1910. Shortly before the turn of the 20th century, CIBA founded its first foreign production site in Pabianice (now in Poland) through a merger with the company Schweikert & Froelich. The town was close to the textile center of Lodz. The plant produced acetic acid and azo and sulfur dyes based on materials fabricated in Basel. Production volumes and the buildings used for manufacture grew continuously until the outbreak of the First World War.

The first direct investments in North America... The USA became Geigy's second most important market after Germany early on. From 1900, American customers were buying goods worth well over 1 million Swiss francs a year, imported via New York. Geigy products were sold through a retail company. In 1903, the newly founded Geigy Aniline & Extract Company, a subsidiary of Geigy Basel, took over distribution. The young company was based at 89 Barclay Street in New York, an ideal address in the heart of an area where many trading and haulage companies, textile firms and banks were based. The dyes manufactured in Basel were distributed by branches in Boston, Philadelphia, Providence and Atlanta in the USA, and Toronto in Canada. In 1904, Geigy set up a mixing plant at an existing factory site in New Jersey, reducing freight costs considerably. The company also set up production facilities for extracts, which could be produced far more profitably in New Jersey than in Basel thanks to the low cost of raw materials.

...and in the UK The Basel-based chemical companies had to import coal tar and the primary products and intermediates derived from it, and did so almost exclusively from Germany. CIBA's largest supplier of products needed for manufacture, Chemische Fabrik Griesheim-Elektron, gradually developed into a synthetic dye producer itself and adopted a very aggressive sales approach. CIBA came under ever greater pressure due to its dependence on the company and tried to free itself from this ruthless competitor. Management decided to acquire a company in the UK in order to secure purchases of products needed for manufacture. In 1911, CIBA acquired the English dye factory Clayton Aniline Company Ltd. in Clayton near Manchester. Sandoz followed suit: on December 8, 1911, The Sandoz Chemical Company Ltd. was entered in the commercial register with a share capital of £2,000. The company began operations at a building in Bradford, although production did not begin until the interwar period. This location was almost preordained, as Sandoz manufactured high-quality wool dyes and Bradford was the center of the prosperous Yorkshire wool industry and the undisputed wool capital of the world.

German chemistry takes a leading role The first dyes were discovered by means of luck, intuition, and trial and error. In the early years of the chemical industry, new dyes and simpler methods of preparation were found using empirical and experimental means. Almost nothing was known about the chemical make-up or structure of dyes. This changed with the birth of structural theory (1858) and benzene theory (1865), both developed by German chemist Friedrich August Kekulé. His work became the basis for the logical development of the whole of dye chemistry. However, only German chemists recognized the full importance of Kekulé's theories, with the French and English paying them little regard. By the end of the 1860s, this was already having an impact: while the early phase of dye chemistry had been dominated by English and French discoveries, German laboratories were now playing the pioneering role. The secret behind their success was simple and effective: an intensive exchange of knowledge between academic chemists and the chemical industry.

Initial innovations from Basel Basel companies initially produced only imitation dyes. As there was no patent protection for chemical processes in Switzerland until 1907, companies based there could copy foreign formulations without any problems. In the 1870s, however, the Basel dye chemistry industry began to market dyes that it had developed itself. In 1894, 15 of the 142 new industrial dyes had been developed by companies in Basel. While Basel was developing far fewer dyes than Germany (with 116), this number still exceeded those made by the English and French (11 in total). The relatively high rate of innovation in the Basel dye industry was partly due to its close relationship with the Federal Polytechnic Institute in Zurich (now the Federal Institute of Technology, Zurich). Chemists with practical training from Zurich played a key role in the Basel industry from the very beginning. Two of them – Bindschedler and Kern – even went on to found their own companies. The innovative successes of Basel companies were based not only on the applicable knowledge of the chemists, however, but also on the process technology expertise of engineers, who had to know the precise setting specifications for equipment and how to distribute temperatures evenly in vessels.

The Basel dye factories move into the pharmaceutical business The modern pharmaceutical industry came into being in the 1880s. In 1884, the German company Farbenwerke Hoechst brought fever-reducing *Antipyrine* on to the market. This quickly became the most successful pharmaceutical product of the century. As there was no patent protection, in 1887 CIBA also began to produce this antipyretic drug. One of the first medications developed in Basel was the anti-inflammatory *Salol,* discovered in 1886 by Professor Marceli Nencki from Bern (Switzerland). Durand & Huguenin acquired the manufacturing rights and brought the active substance to market as an antirheumatic. In 1895, Sandoz also began manufacture of its first pharmaceutical product: by joining the Antipyrine Agreement, the company secured itself a fixed portion of the business coordinated and managed by Hoechst. In addition to *Antipyrine*, Sandoz also produced and successfully marketed synthetic saccharine and plant-based codeine that had been developed and launched by German companies. The oldest Basel dye factory, Geigy, felt obliged to pursue a conservative business policy until the outbreak of the First World War, and ruled out entering the pharmaceutical sector. By contrast, the youngest company, Basler Chemische Fabrik (BCF), produced both dyes and pharmaceuticals from the outset. In the last financial year before its merger with CIBA, BCF generated 2.5 million Swiss francs from sales of dyes and medicinal products. Its pharmaceutical business accounted for 40 per cent of total sales — significantly higher than at CIBA, which generated only 7 per cent of its total sales in this sector. Through its acquisition of BCF, CIBA also gained access to interesting pharmaceutical products, including the antiseptic *Vioform* and the antirheumatic *Salen*.

Pharmaceutical competition in Basel: the founding of Roche In 1896, Fritz Hoffmann-La Roche (1868–1920) founded a company in Basel devoted exclusively to the manufacture and trading of pharmaceutical products. Hoffmann-La Roche was neither a pharmacist nor a physician, as was usual for founders of drug companies, but a proactive young businessman. The company soon expanded abroad (to Milan in 1897, Paris in 1903 and New York in 1905). Until the outbreak of the First World War, it generated sales primarily from *Sirolin*, a cough medicine launched in 1898. Its orange flavor and clever advertising quickly made this product a bestseller.

Geigy Karavayevka (Russia).
Left: Carl Koechlin-Iselin
(1856-1914), head and part owner
of Geigy; right: Jakob Emil
Zehnder, technical head of the
Russian factory. Probably 1900.

Geigy Karavayevka.
Foreground, right: the Russian
factory coachman; left,
wearing fur hat: J. E. Zehnder,
technical head of the factory.
Probably 1900.

012

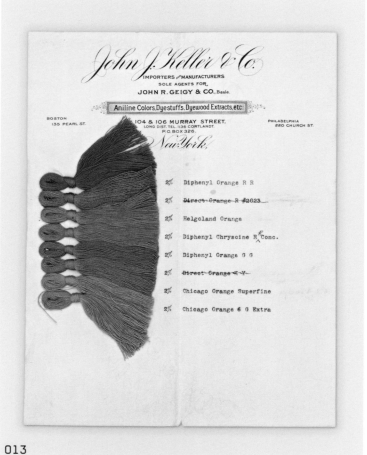

013

012
Vioform powder dispenser (CIBA). 1920s.

013
Sample card of Geigy's US agent
John J. Keller & Co., New York. Around 1900.

014
Aerial photograph of the Geigy plant,
Grenzach (Germany). 1924.

014

Geigy Basel. Dye works.
Around 1900.

CIBA Basel. Accounting department.
July 14, 1909.

CIBA Basel. Middle boiler houses.
1911.

CIBA Basel. Business Management
office. Standing: Heinrich Hollen-
weger (1852–1926), sitting: German
Georg (1862–1911). 1910.

015

Traugott Sandmeyer (1854–1922). 1897.
Traugott Sandmeyer, born in Wettingen
(Switzerland), completed an apprenticeship
in precision engineering in Zurich.
He went on to teach himself chemistry.
In 1882, Professor Victor Meyer, who had
recognized Sandmeyer's extraordinary gift
for chemistry, created an assistant post
at the Federal Polytechnic Institute in Zurich
especially for him. There, in 1884, Sandmeyer
discovered the Sandmeyer reaction, which
was named after him. In 1888, he joined
Geigy, where he made numerous important
discoveries on the synthesis of dyes
and their associated products. His work had
lasting benefits for the global growth of
Geigy. Sandmeyer was awarded an honorary
doctorate by the University of Heidelberg
(Germany) in 1891, and in 1915 was made
Doctor *honoris causa* of the Federal Institute
of Technology, Zurich.

016

**CIBA production facilities, Pabianice
(Russia before the First World War;
now Poland). 1930s.**

017

**Works entrance to Clayton Aniline & Co. Ltd.
in Clayton near Manchester (England). 1953.**

015

Sandoz Basel. Chemists
Oskar Knecht, Heinrich Fulda
(sitting on chair) and
Alfred Raillard (right, standing).
May 14, 1910.

CIBA Pabianice (Russia, now
Poland). Factory fire department.
Around 1910.

CIBA Basel. Repair center. 1911.

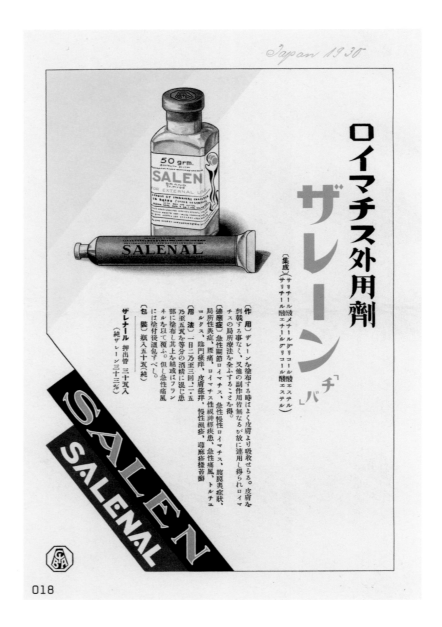

018

018
Japanese brochure for *Salen* (CIBA). 1930.

019
**Gas absorption system from the 1880s
at the Geigy Rosental plant in Basel. 1944.**

019

CIBA Basel. Workers from the
Pharmaceutical department. 1911.

Geigy manager for the Indian
dye business, Walter Sänger,
with Indian agents. 1912.

020
**Geigy production facilities, Karavayevka,
near Moscow (Russia). Probably 1900.**

021
**CIBA industrial plant, Saint-Fons, near Lyon
(France). Around 1910.**

022
Pump at the Geigy Rosental site. 1893.
This photograph of a suction pump is taken
from an old photo album and is entitled
"Master Hiltbold and his pump, 1893".
The mechanic Abraham Hiltpold, seen on
the right, designed the system himself.
It pumped water from a canal into the Rosen-
tal reservoir. It was dismantled on May 22,
1919.

022

3 THE FIRST WORLD WAR

HOLDING FIRM IN TROUBLED TIMES
1914–1918

Historians describe the First World War as the seminal catastrophe of the 20th century. Millions died in the first "industrial war" and the previously stable global trading system collapsed abruptly. The First World War destroyed the old order and the traditional power structure in Europe. Three empires collapsed: the German Reich, the Austro-Hungarian monarchy and the Czarist empire. Two new superpowers with conflicting social systems emerged: the USA and the Soviet Union. However, states whose neutrality was respected – the Scandinavian countries, the Netherlands and Switzerland – were not so affected by the war. They even gained some economic advantages from it.

Record profits thanks to loss of competition When hostilities broke out in August 1914, the head offices of the Basel companies were anxious and bewildered. There were no indications that the Basel chemical industry would soon be posting record profits. Half of all production workers and three-quarters of chemists employed by CIBA had to join the army. But the First World War fundamentally changed economic conditions in favor of neutral Switzerland. On the eve of the war, the global market for textile dyestuffs was almost exclusively the preserve of German and Swiss companies. Germany manufactured around 85 per cent of textile dyestuffs, and Basel around 10 per cent. The outbreak of the war changed these market shares almost overnight. The Germans suspended their exports, and the British and French were unable in the short term to compensate by expanding their own industries. The British and French therefore turned instead to the Basel chemical companies, whose dyestuffs were primarily needed for uniforms. The absence of previously overwhelming German competition from the markets of Germany's enemies opened up unprecedented opportunities for Swiss dyestuff manufacturers – albeit to varying degrees. CIBA made the strongest gains in absolute terms, and Geigy the weakest. In relative terms, Sandoz was the biggest winner: its turnover in 1914 was 6 million Swiss francs (of which 10 per cent was from pharmaceutical products), but this had already increased to over 14 million Swiss francs by 1915. Management's annual report to the Board of Directors stated: "Sales went very smoothly; everything we could produce was taken off our hands immediately." Sales by Sandoz rocketed the following year to almost 30 million Swiss francs, and rose in the last two years of the war to 37 million Swiss francs. The largest purchaser by far was the UK textile industry, which was the industry leader at the time. In 1917, Sandoz exported some 40 per cent of its dyestuffs to the UK. Other sales markets included the USA (22 per cent), Italy (13 per cent), Switzerland and Japan (each 5 per cent), China (4.4 per cent), France (4.3 per cent) and Spain (3.4 per cent).

War profits on the one hand, loss of real wages on the other The dramatic increase in sales of Basel dye chemicals during the war, together with the extraordinarily high dividends and royalties, caused widespread resentment in the population. Whereas large numbers of people were becoming increasingly desperate due to the enormous rise in the cost of living and the inadequate adjustment of wages for inflation, shareholders, members of the boards and directors were treated extremely generously. In contrast to the local dyeworks and textile factories, in the Basel chemical companies there were only minor and temporary losses of purchasing power. An investigation published in 2014 for Geigy (see bibliography) suggests that cost-of-living increases were indeed delayed, but when they came they reflected inflation reasonably, though the megaprofits were of course not distributed. On the other hand, towards the end of the war the chemicals companies poured a great deal of money into support and pension funds for workers, chemists and staff.

Sandoz establishes in-house pharmaceutical research The establishment of independent pharmaceutical research at Sandoz is a milestone in the history of the predecessor companies of Novartis. The initiator of this move was presumably Sandoz Director Melchior Böniger (1866–1929): in 1915, he asked Professor Robert Gnehm (1852–1926) to find a competent person who could establish a pharmaceutical department in his company. As a former Director and member of the Board of Directors of CIBA and the former Chairman of the Board of Directors of Sandoz, Gnehm was very familiar with the chemical industry. Furthermore, as Chairman of the Swiss School Board (now the ETH Board) and a former Professor at and Director of the Federal Polytechnic Institute in Zurich, he had a good insight into research and knew the reputations of individual scientists. At Gnehm's suggestion, the Board of Directors of Sandoz appointed Swiss chemist Arthur Stoll (1887–1971) on March 15, 1917. In hindsight, this landmark decision seems both farsighted and carefully considered. However, in the context of the time, it was hardly either of these, as Sandoz lacked experience in this area. Profits were also only expected in the medium term. The decision was assuredly not a strategic one: the matter came up under "Any Other Business" and was approved without discussion. Everything indicates that the members of the Board did not realize the import of their decision.

The company had succeeded in attracting a high-ranking scientist in Stoll. He had worked closely with Nobel Laureate Richard Willstätter, first in Zurich, and then in Berlin (Germany) and Munich (Germany). Stoll had made the area of chlorophyll research his own and gained new insights there. For these achievements, he was awarded the title of Royal Bavarian Professor in 1917 on Willstätter's recommendation. From the outset, Stoll focused the research programme of the new Sandoz department on highly effective natural remedies. He aimed to isolate their active substances in pure form, and to manufacture medications from them that could be precisely dosed and were consistently effective. It had long been known in traditional medicine that plants such as belladonna and foxglove had healing properties, but extracts from medicinal plants at that time were usually not pure enough, did not keep well and were often unpredictable. Dosages had to be based on instinct and their effectiveness was inconsistent. Stoll's first study involved ergot (*Secale cornutum*). This growth on rye and wild grasses, caused by a fungus (*Claviceps purpurea*), had been used since the Middle Ages to induce childbirth. In 1918, using a new process that he had helped to develop in Willstätter's laboratory, Stoll was able to isolate a crystalline alkaloid which he called ergotamine. Working together with pharmacologists and clinicians, he was able to prove that ergotamine is the active substance in ergot. Three years later, ergotamine was launched under the brand name *Gynergen* as a drug to staunch the dreaded postpartum haemorrhages. However, the innovative isolation process was to prove more important than this novel product itself for the further development of the pharmaceutical department: the process could be transferred to other areas, such as belladonna alkaloids and cardioactive glycosides. Management at Sandoz recognized the potential of the discovery and patented the "Procedure to isolate a high-quality product from *Secale cornutum*" in April 1918 with the Swiss Federal Institute for Intellectual Property.

Geigy Basel. Soccer players
from the FC Geigy team, founded
in 1920. 1920.

Geigy Basel. Vehicle fleet.
May 24, 1919.

Geigy Basel: "Tribelhörner"
(Swiss vehicles with electric
motors) and trucks driving
through the Rosental site.
May 24, 1919.

023

Robert Gnehm (1852–1926). Around 1910.
Robert Gnehm, born in the small Swiss town
of Stein am Rhein, graduated in technical
chemistry from the Federal Polytechnic
Institute, Zurich, in 1872. There he met Alfred
Kern, with whom he would remain friends
until Kern's untimely death. While Kern
moved into practice after his studies, Gnehm
stayed at the Federal Polytechnic Institute,
gained a postdoctoral qualification and was
made a professor in 1876. However, in 1877,
he decided to leave Zurich and followed
his friend to the Karl Oehler dyestuff factory
in Offenbach (Germany). Both men returned
to Switzerland the following year, with
Gnehm heading first to Schwanden and then
in 1880 to Basel, to the Bindschedler & Busch
aniline dyestuff factory. When the company
became CIBA in 1884, he was appointed
a member of management. In 1892, he was
elected to the Board of Directors, but
stepped down in 1894. That same year, Gnehm
was appointed Professor for Technical
Chemistry at the Federal Polytechnic Institute, Zurich. In 1895, he joined the Board
of Directors of Sandoz, and was its Chairman
from 1896 to 1900.

024

**Steam engine in building 34 at the Geigy
plant, Basel. June 20, 1920.**

023

Geigy Basel. Staff of building 21.
October 2, 1919.

Sandoz Basel. The first chef of
the Sandoz canteen with his staff.
Around 1920.

025
**Spanish rail pass for Melchior Böniger
(1866–1929) and Ida Böniger-Ris. 1926.**
Melchior Böniger, born in Nidfurn
in the Swiss Canton of Glarus, completed
his studies in natural sciences at the
Federal Polytechnic Institute, Zurich,
in 1888. He gained his doctorate at the
University of Zurich in 1889, and joined
Sandoz in the same year as a chemist.
Böniger was a director there from 1895
to 1921; in 1922, he was elected to the
company's Board of Directors. Sandoz
is indebted to him for the decisive course
taken to develop in-house pharmaceutical
research. Böniger supported welfare
institutions for production and office
workers and was involved in a number of
committees on economic policy.

026
Gynergen packaging. 1930s.

027
Arthur Stoll (1887–1971). Around 1930.
Arthur Stoll was born in Schinznach-Dorf
(Switzerland). He studied natural sciences at
the Federal Polytechnic Institute in
Zurich from 1906, where he became an assistant to Professor Richard Willstätter.
He completed his doctorate in 1911. When
Willstätter was appointed to the Kaiser Wil-
helm Institute of Chemistry in Berlin-Dahlem
in 1912, Stoll went with him as his senior
assistant. Four years later, he followed his
teacher to Munich (Germany). In 1917, Stoll
was awarded the title of Royal Bavarian
Professor. That same year, Sandoz entrusted
him with the task of setting up the pharmaceutical research department. He quickly
achieved scientific success with products
based on ergot and cardioactive natural substances. At the same time, he built up a sales
and advertising organization. Stoll became
a Director of Sandoz in 1923, and was a member of the Board of Directors and CEO
of Sandoz from 1933 to 1963. Stoll received
numerous awards, including the Marcel
Benoist Prize in 1942 and the Paul Karrer
Medal in 1959. He was also awarded 18 honorary doctorates.

025

026

027

ERGOT ALKALOIDS

Medicines from a fungus

1
Ergot products. Probably 1980s.

2
Board seeding. 1942.

3
Delivery of ergot in Aefligen, Emmental (Canton of Berne). October 6, 1967. Ergot occurring naturally in Switzerland was chiefly collected in Emmental. By the end of the 1930s at the latest, the deliveries from Emmental were no longer sufficient to meet the enormous demand for ergot preparations. Consequently, farmers in rural Lucerne, together with others in Freiburg, Grisons and Solothurn, also began to grow ergot for Sandoz. Whereas in 1939 just 3,500 kilograms of ergot were produced, in 1954 it was reported to be already 484,800 kilograms.

The young pharmaceutical department of Sandoz isolated the active substances from known medicinal plants in pure form and used them to produce medicines with precise dosages. Using this successful technique, Arthur Stoll managed to isolate the highly active substance ergotamine in pure form in 1918. This ergot alkaloid was launched on the market under the name *Gynergen* in 1921. After initially being used to stop postnatal bleeding, thereby saving many women's lives, a further application as a remedy for migraines was added in the late 1920s.

Ergot alkaloids are natural substances produced by the fungus *Claviceps purpurea*. This sac fungus is parasitic, living primarily on rye. It invades the ovary of its host plant and forms a violet-black sclerotium which protrudes from the plant's spikes. This protruding growth contains alkaloids and is also known as ergot (*Secale cornutum*). Cereals infected by this fungus must not be eaten. If consumed in large quantities, ergot causes poisoning. "Ignis sacer" (holy fire) or "Saint Anthony's fire" were medieval terms for ergotism, the symptoms of poisoning by infected crops. In those days, mass poisonings caused by ergot alkaloids were not uncommon.

The first precise description of ergot can be found in the *Kräuterbuch*, published in 1582 by Adam Lonitzer, botanist and town physician of Frankfurt am Main (Germany). Lonitzer looked on ergot primarily as a medicine and knew that midwives used it to induce labor. The first chemical experiments to isolate the active substances in ergot were performed in the 19th century: in 1875, Frenchman Charles Tanret extracted a crystalline mixture of three alkaloids from ergot, calling it ergotinine. This compound did not gain acceptance in medical practice, however. English chemists George Barger and Francis Howard Carr managed to isolate a mixture known as ergotoxin in 1907. This did have a certain physiological effect, but was not strong enough to be used for treatment purposes. Stoll, therefore, was able to build on an existing tradition of research into ergot.

With the isolation of ergotamine in 1918, Stoll laid the foundations for systematic research into ergot at Sandoz. In the late 1930s, Sandoz chemists succeeded in partially synthesizing the natural ergot alkaloids. They began varying the chemical structure and, consequently, the pharmacological effects, which opened up new areas of application. The substances were used to treat disorders of the vegetative nervous system (*Bellergal*), age-related symptoms of cerebral insufficiency (*Hydergin*), hypotonic circulatory disorders (*Dihydergot*) and tension headaches (*Cafergot, Deseril*). They were also prescribed as a prophylactic against postoperative thromboembolisms (*Heparin-Dihydergot*). When the product *Parlodel/Pravidel* was launched in the 1970s, it attracted considerable scientific attention: the partially synthesized ergot alkaloid it contained, bromocriptine, was the first in a new class of medicines which stimulated dopamine receptors. Today, the dopamine agonist *Parlodel* is still used in the treatment of a range of disorders such as hyperprolactinemia (abnormally high prolactin concentrations in the blood), Parkinson's disease and acromegaly.

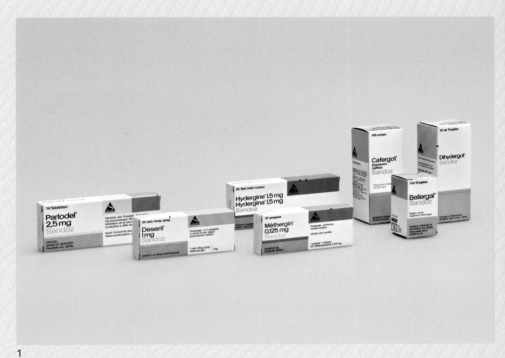

1

2

3

4

THE INTERWAR PERIOD

A BOOM IN PHARMACEUTICALS
1918–1939

The First World War brought an end to the era of free trade. Protectionism took hold of the global economy. Many countries either introduced tariff protection for the first time or increased their tariffs. Trade barriers ranged from export and import licenses to import quotas and bans to foreign currency controls. A protectionist mentality became widespread during the 1920s to an extent previously unheard of. It affected not only mass-produced commodities, but also specialist and high-quality goods. The Swiss chemical industry had to adapt to this development. The Great Depression hit in 1929, marking a low point in international trade relations.

Tackling the new competition: the founding of Basler IG The end of the war changed market conditions at a stroke. The victorious allies, in particular the UK and the USA, had developed their own chemical industries in the interim, and these were now penetrating the international market. In response to this, the Basel dyestuff producers closed ranks: CIBA, Sandoz and Geigy formed an interest group in September 1918 known as Basler IG. Unlike the German dyestuff manufacturers that merged to form IG Farben in 1925, the companies in Basler IG retained their independence. The aim of the interest group was to strengthen the Basel companies in an increasingly competitive environment. The companies centralized and rationalized, operated a collective purchasing policy and established joint production sites: one such was built in Cincinnati (Ohio, USA) in 1920, and another in Seriate (near Bergamo, Italy) in 1925. To avoid internal competition, the three companies divided specific areas of research and production between themselves. They agreed to pool all profits, which were then still largely generated from dyestuffs, and distribute them between themselves based on fixed proportions. After initial difficulties regarding the distribution formula, they agreed on the following: from 1920 onwards, 52 per cent of total annual profits would be allocated to CIBA, and 24 per cent each to Geigy and Sandoz. This basically continued to apply until Basler IG disbanded prematurely at the end of 1950. While Geigy and Sandoz generated similar profits in the late 1920s, the proportion contributed by Geigy fell steadily during the 1930s: in 1939, it accounted for only 14.5 per cent of the group's income. As the weakest partner, Geigy therefore benefited from the profit-sharing arrangement, which led to continual conflicts between the three companies.

Pharmaceuticals gain in importance Why did the development in the IG partners' profits vary so greatly? The key reason lay in their differing structures: when Basler IG was founded, CIBA and Sandoz secured the areas of vat dyestuffs and alizarin for themselves, which brought them considerable success. In addition, they had exclusive rights to pharmaceutical production, as they had already established corresponding departments before Basler IG was founded. By contrast, Geigy only started to set up a pharmaceutical department in 1938. Pharmaceutical products in particular proved to be highly profitable and experienced considerable growth in the interwar period. Thus, in 1934, Sandoz managed to sell 14 per cent more pharmaceutical specialty products than it did the previous year, and sales of specialty products continued to develop very positively in the subsequent years. Sandoz regularly launched new products and took a great deal of care over their marketing, to good effect: in 1935, sales rose by 22.5 per cent. At its meeting on March 25, 1936, the Board of Directors was proud to note that the Sandoz pharmaceutical business "has already reached 55 per cent of CIBA's business". In 1938, sales of pharmaceutical specialty products rose again by 13.5 per cent over the previous year, achieving around half the sales reported for dyestuffs. At this time, Germany was the most important customer for Sandoz pharmaceuticals, with around a 30 per cent share of total sales.

Hormones at CIBA… Prior to the First World War, CIBA manufactured three categories of products: the first group included pure substances (e.g. the iodine product *Lipojodin*); the second, standardized extracts from animal (e.g. the blood-clotting product *Coagulen*) and plant substances (e.g. the cardiac medication *Digifolin*); and the third, synthetic products (e.g. the sleep medication and sedative *Dial*). During the war, CIBA decided to move into an area with promising future prospects: between 1918 and 1939, the company launched eight gonadal and hormone products. The oldest products, *Agomensin* and *Sistomensin*, were used to treat menstrual disorders. In 1927, CIBA launched *Prokliman* to treat the symptoms of menopause. This was followed in 1931 by *Androstin*, which targeted "climacterium virile", or the male menopause, and impotence. These four products were purified extracts from the female and male gonads, rather than pure sex hormones. CIBA scientists achieved synthesis or "artificial" manufacture of human sex hormones in the mid-1930s. *Perandren* was launched in 1936, followed by *Ovocyclin* and *Lutocyclin* in 1938 – all three were synthetic hormone products. From 1939, CIBA marketed *Percorten*, the first synthetic hormone product to replace the natural substances produced by the adrenal cortex. It was prescribed for adrenocortical insufficiency.

… and calcium at Sandoz Since its foundation during the First World War, the young pharmaceutical department at Sandoz had been growing slowly but steadily. Within five years, it had launched four medications. However, it was still costing the company money rather than turning a profit. At the meeting of the Board of Directors on May 12, 1922, Albert His-Veillon (1858–1935) remarked that "a number of very good specialty products" were being sold, but that the department "still [had] no money-spinner"; he said that the pharmaceutical department should "now turn its attention to developing this type of profitable product". The pharmaceutical department finally turned a profit in 1924, albeit only 27,000 Swiss francs. Nevertheless, Arthur Stoll noted with satisfaction at the Board meeting of April 30, 1925, that "this area of the business has been able to cover its own costs for the first time". Stoll had worked consistently towards an effective advertising organization and an efficient distribution system. His efforts were now bearing fruit. From 1927, the company also had a bestseller, in the form of *Calcium-Sandoz*. By 1929, this product to treat calcium deficiency and related disorders had become the best-selling Sandoz pharmaceutical product. On average, *Calcium-Sandoz* accounted for over one-third of sales in the first half of the 1930s.

Specialization, diversification and internationalization The Basel companies specialized their dyestuff production during the interwar period. They focused on a wide range of high-value products, particularly patented specialties. This enabled them to offset losses from older classes of dyestuffs, where foreign competitors dominated. The Basel chemical industry also moved into new areas: it no longer only produced dyestuffs and medications, but also textile auxiliary substances, textile finishing products (e.g. wetting and leveling agents and fluorescent whitening agents), plastics, cosmetics and pesticides. The Basel chemical industry founded further foreign subsidiaries in the interwar period, and set up new production sites abroad: in the USA, the UK, Japan, Spain, Belgium, Italy, Canada, France, Germany, Czechoslovakia, Argentina, Brazil, China and Portugal. These foreign investments were made in order to increase competitiveness through lower production and transport costs, circumvent import restrictions and obstacles to market entry, gain greater proximity to customers and tap new markets.

Expansion of the Basel sites Thanks to their sensational performances, CIBA and Sandoz were able to start modernizing their Basel sites and expanding their production facilities even during the First World War. This continued during the 1920s and 1930s. The old production sheds at the Sandoz St. Johann site gave way to multistorey manufacturing premises. According to a contemporary Swiss architectural journal, the new industrial buildings "[took] into account the challenges of our time" by making allowance for "the demand for beauty in their external appearance, and the demand for efficacy as regards the interior". The buildings were designed by Ernst Eckenstein, the company's in-house architect from 1915 to 1939. His final project at the St. Johann site was the construction of the new administration building designed by architects Brodtbeck & Bohny. After the Second World War, this angular building (later known as building 200, now Forum 1) was extended by two new wings to make it rectangular.

Chemotextil AG in Lovosice
(Czechoslovakia, now the Czech
Republic), a Sandoz holding.
Packaging unit for sucrose.
End of the 1930s.

Geigy Basel. Dyeworks. April 1937.

Sandoz Basel. Ampoule filling.
Early 1930s.

028

028
Digifolin packaging (CIBA). 1920s.

029
Norwood production facilities for azo
dyestuffs at the joint plant in Cincinnati
(Ohio, USA). 1938.

030
Administration building at the joint plant
in Seriate near Bergamo (Italy). 1939.

029

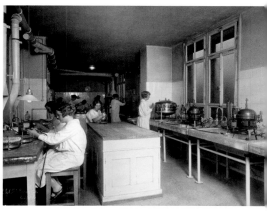

030

CIBA Saint-Fons near Lyon
(France).
Correspondence office.
February 24, 1926.

CIBA Brussels (Belgium).
Laboratory. January 1938.

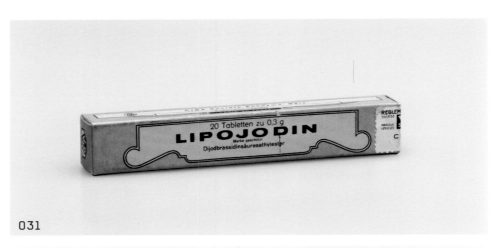

031

031
Lipojodin packaging (CIBA). 1930s.

032
Coramin advertising blotter. 1925.
Coramin was launched in 1924.
This respiratory and circulatory stimulant
was among other things used for reviving
people who had suffered drowning.
It remained a key sales driver for CIBA for
decades.

033
Basel production facility for *Calcium-
Sandoz*. Early 1930s.

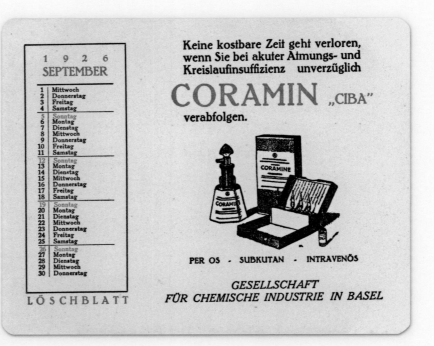

032

033

034

034
Advertising poster for CIBA Binaca tooth-paste. 1941. © 2012 Pro Litteris, Zurich.
Painter and graphic designer Niklaus
Stoecklin restricted himself to the key
message in this masterpiece of Swiss
poster art: a glass, a tube of toothpaste
and a toothbrush – strikingly plastic.

035
**Rear of Sandoz Chemical Works, Inc. in
Charlton Street, New York. 1930s.**
The US subsidiary of Sandoz was founded
on July 16, 1919. Alongside import and sales,
the commercial register entry already
mentions production of dyestuffs, chemicals
and pharmaceutical products.

036
**Warehouse of the Geigy Colour Company Ltd.,
Manchester (UK). Around 1925.**

035

036

Sandoz Basel. Filling of *Optalidon* suppositories. Prior to 1939.

CIBA Chicago. July 1920.

CIBA Philadelphia (Pennsylvania, USA). July 1920.

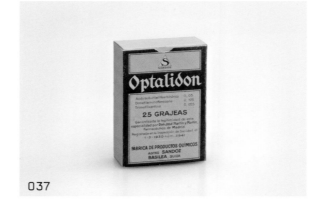

037

037
***Optalidon* packaging. Probably 1930s.**
Sandoptal, a barbituric acid derivative launched in 1927, was Sandoz's first step into the field of synthetic medicines. Despite being highly effective, the drug never became properly established. Apart from the barbituric acid derivative marketed by the German companies Merck and Bayer under the generic name of *Veronal*, many other barbiturates had been available for some time. Sandoz had more success with *Optalidon,* a combination drug created from *Sandoptal,* pyramidon and caffeine, which was launched in 1928. This drug was highly successful with dentists in particular, although many other pain-relief products were already available.

038
CIBA Charlotte (North Carolina, USA). 1920s.

039
CIBA Chicago. Secretariat. 1938.

038

Geigy Basel. Site fire department.
October 1932.

CIBA Prague (Czechoslovakia,
now the Czech Republic).
Storage facility. January 1938.

CIBA Bombay (now Mumbai, India).
Dyeworks laboratory. January 1938.

040
**Storage facility for intermediate products
at the Sandoz site in Basel. Early 1930s.**

041
**Dining room in the welfare building at the
Sandoz site in Basel. Early 1930s.**

Feuerwehr J.-R. Geigy A.-G.
— 1932 —

041

Sandoz Basel. Ampoule filling.
Before 1939.

Sandoz Basel. Label storage
facility of the pharmaceutical
packaging department.
Before 1939.

Sandoz Basel. Ampoule cartoning
of *Calcium-Sandoz*. Before 1939.

042
**Construction of the new administration
building at the Sandoz site in Basel.
March 2, 1938.**

043
**Administration building at the Sandoz site
in Basel. 1943.**

043

CIBA Osaka (Japan). January 1938.

CIBA Osaka. Elbon packing area. 1927.

CIBA Osaka. Advertising department. 1927.

CIBA Osaka. Scientific office and sales organization. January 1938.

044

044
Elbon packaging. Probably 1930s.
The first scientific publication on the treatment of tubercular fever with Elbon, a cinnamic acid product launched by CIBA, appeared in 1911.

045 | 046
Tuberculosis Day in Osaka. 1927.
Nurses distribute brochures about the tuberculosis drug Elbon.

045

Correspondence office of CIBA
Shanghai (China). Probably 1938.

Laboratory of CIBA Shanghai.
Probably 1938.

047
Premises of CIBA Shanghai. Around 1938.

048
**Accounting office of CIBA Shanghai.
Probably 1938.**

048

EARLY HORMONE PRODUCTS FROM CIBA

First from animals,
then from the laboratory

At the beginning of the 20th century, various physiologists, biologists and physicians suspected that the gonads – in other words, the ovaries and the testes – produced chemical substances which are distributed throughout the body via the blood. Three decades later, these substances were given the name "sex hormones". By the mid-1930s, the five most important sex hormones had been isolated, synthesized and given the names by which we know them today: estrone, estradiol, progesterone, androsterone and testosterone. The pharmaceutical industry played a leading role in research into sex hormones. In Switzerland, CIBA in particular dedicated itself intensively and persistently to research into sex hormones from 1914 onwards, and in the interwar period, the company launched seven different hormone products as patented medicinal product innovations. In 1918, CIBA had launched its first two extracts from animal ovaries: *Agomensin* and *Sistomensin*, which were mainly used to treat menstrual disorders. Although both were patent-protected original CIBA products, the manufacturing processes had been discovered by external scientists who had sold them to the Basel-based company. By contrast *Prokliman*, launched in 1927, and *Androstin*, available from 1931, were based on processes which the CIBA laboratory had been using for some time to manufacture organ extracts. *Prokliman* was a combination drug: alongside the ovary extract, it also contained a laxative, a sedative, a vasodilator and a blood pressure regulator. It promised to alleviate the symptoms of the female menopause. *Androstin*, a testicular extract, was also aimed at treating climacteric complaints, namely problems caused by the "male menopause".

CIBA worked on synthesizing sex hormones from the 1920s. A number of advantages were expected to result from synthetic replacements for hormone extracts. Raw material procurement would be simplified, meaning that production quantities would not be dependent on the availability of slaughterhouse waste – partly imported from South America. Furthermore, synthetic production methods were considered to be much more reliable in terms of purity and effectiveness than traditional extraction processes. From 1935 onwards, CIBA scientists were not only able to manufacture natural sex hormones by partial synthesis. They also managed to construct sex hormones which do not occur in nature, but are far more effective than their natural prototypes. This new knowledge was the result of various forms of cooperation. The key factor was the collaboration with Professor Leopold Ružička of the Federal Institute of Technology, Zurich. In 1932, Ružička presented a plan for manufacturing synthetic hormones by means of partial synthesis. In just two years, his university research team in Zurich managed to artificially create the male hormone androsterone from cholesterol. Meanwhile, industrial chemists in Basel developed a method for isolating the hormone progesterone in crystallized form from animal ovaries. In 1935, Ružička was able to announce – together with CIBA chemist Albert Wettstein (1907–1974) – that he had worked out the chemical structure of the male hormone testosterone. The following year, CIBA launched its first synthetic hormone: *Perandren*. This was followed in 1938 by *Ovocyclin* and *Lutocyclin*, CIBA's first synthetic female hormones. The active substance in *Perandren* was a testosterone derivative with a chemical structure that does not occur in nature. *Ovocyclin*, too, was based on a synthetic hormone, an artificial estradiol compound. *Lutocyclin's* active substance was synthetic progesterone. At the same time, Tadeusz Reichstein from the Federal Institute of Technology was researching the hormones secreted by the adrenal cortex. He obtained the organ extracts from Dutch pharmaceutical company Organon. In 1936, Reichstein was able to show that, like sex hormones, substances from the adrenal cortex (corticosteroids) are also steroids. CIBA was keen to prevent knowledge about the structure of steroid hormones reaching foreign competitors via Reichstein. Conversely, Reichstein and Organon had little choice but to continue working with CIBA, as the company held important patents in the field of steroids. In 1939, CIBA launched the first synthetic adrenal cortex product under the trade name *Percorten*, which was initially prescribed to treat Addison's disease (adrenal insufficiency).

The seven gonadal and hormone products together with *Percorten* remained on the market under various identities – new combinations, manufacturing processes and indications – until the 1950s and 1960s.

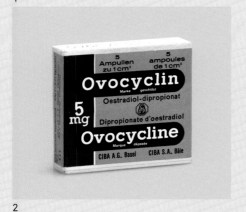

1

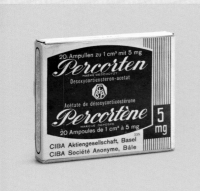

2

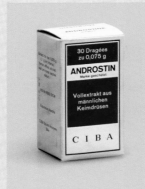

3

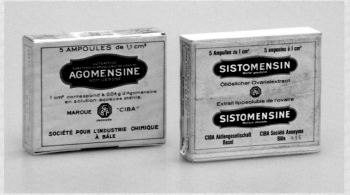

4

5

CALCIUM-SANDOZ

The cornerstone of modern calcium therapy

Calcium was used in China as a haemostatic as early as the pre-Christian era. In the 16th century, the famous doctor, alchemist and philosopher Paracelsus prescribed a compound made from calcium-rich corals for uterine haemorrhage. The scientific principles behind calcium therapy were first established in the 1890s, and the first quarter of the 20th century saw the launch of numerous calcium products on the market. They were used for a broad range of indications, including hives, rickets, scrofula, as a tonic during pregnancy and as a prophylactic against catarrh. In 1924, German pediatrician Kurt Blühdorn observed jokingly that "there is hardly a disease for which chalk has not been used as a treatment". The calcium products were based on a range of salts, combinations and dosage forms. However, the calcium therapy of the day had a number of problems to contend with. If administered by injection, calcium was poorly tolerated, often leading to painful tissue injuries which were slow to heal. By contrast, orally administered calcium chloride, which was the most common product of that time, had a harsh, salty and bitter taste and often caused indigestion. Patients would usually refuse to continue taking it after a short while. The turnaround came with the launch of *Calcium-Sandoz* in 1927: made from calcium gluconate – an organic salt compound chemically derived from glucose – this product was completely taste-neutral, which gave it a considerable advantage over the other calcium salts. Of even greater importance was the fact that, in contrast to competitor products, *Calcium-Sandoz* had a very high tissue tolerance. Sandoz also emphasized the storage effect which occurred when the salt compound was injected intramuscularly.

Calcium-Sandoz turned out to be a stroke of luck for the company. Although the pharmaceutical department founded in 1917 soon enjoyed scientific success with products based on ergot and cardioactive natural substances, the market was slow to embrace the new medicines. First, the new specialties did not address the needs of the masses, such as treatments for fever and coughs, and were focused on narrow indication areas. Second, Sandoz was still a relatively unknown brand. This meant that, initially, the pharmaceutical department only generated costs. In 1919, company founder Edouard Sandoz accused it of causing a "useless increase in expenses". And its head, Arthur Stoll, soon became known as the "expenses director", while his colleague in the dyestuffs department was considered the "income director". The pharmaceutical department only became profitable in 1924. However, even then the small profit of 27,000 Swiss francs did not come from its pharmaceutical specialties (i.e. its own, patented inventions, which still generated a loss of over 300,000 Swiss francs), but from strong sales in the alkaloid business (trade in active substances). Pharmaceutical specialties were only catapulted into the profit zone when *Calcium-Sandoz* was launched on the market. As the salt of an alkaline earth metal, it may have been anything but a "fine product" based on "physiologically specific active substances from the plant and animal kingdom": it was dosed in grams and manufactured by the tonne. But *Calcium-*

1
Calcium-Sandoz tin. 1930s.

2
Packaging of *Calcium-Sandoz* for intramuscular and intravenous injection and a sample pack of *Calcium-Sandoz + Vitamin C*. 1980s.

3
Brochure for *Calcium-Sandoz with Vitamin C*. 1950.

1

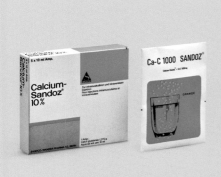

2

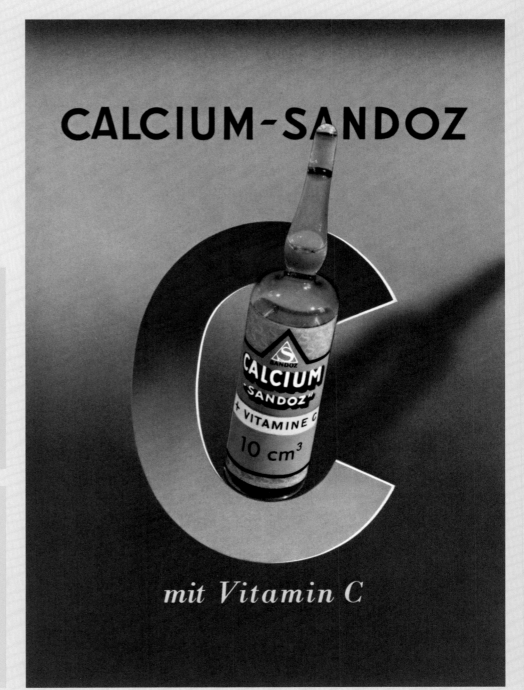

3

4
Sandoz Basel. Filling calcium granules.
Prior to 1939.

5
Sandoz Basel. Preparing *Calcium-Sandoz*
chocolate tablets. Prior to 1939.

Sandoz was a resounding market success, growing to become the company's best-selling medicine by 1929. It became synonymous with calcium therapy and turned the company into a household name. In the following decades, Sandoz continuously expanded its range of calcium products. While previous applications such as the treatment of tetany, bronchial asthma, hay fever and bronchitis gradually faded into the background, the product became increasingly important as a prophylactic against osteoporosis.

4

5

5 THE SECOND WORLD WAR AND THE EARLY POSTWAR PERIOD

STAGNATION AND MODERNIZATION
1939–1951

The Second World War is considered one of the bloodiest conflicts in history. After Italy had joined the war and France was defeated in June 1940, Switzerland was almost totally surrounded by the Axis powers. Following the occupation of Southern France in the fall of 1942, its isolation was complete. This was a new situation for Switzerland. Its economy – closely interwoven with international markets and dependent both on exports of goods and services and imports of raw materials and food – was now cut off from the world market.

The Basel chemical industry – isolated, but well equipped Unlike in 1914, the Basel chemical companies were already well established when the Second World War broke out in September 1939. In the interwar period they had undergone significant geographic expansion, entered new sectors and launched new products. With the outbreak of war, foreign branches and production sites became even more important. To some extent, they enabled the isolated Basel headquarters to continue to serve the international markets and maintain key customer relationships. Sales of medicines, chemicals and pesticides performed well, which made up for losses in the dyestuffs sector. In 1939, the Basel companies' dyestuff business had recorded improved sales figures in its markets thanks to precautionary buying and stockpiling. During the course of the war, however, sales quickly fell below the figures for the 1930s. As the key industrial nations were producing fewer fashionable textiles, demand for dyes slumped. In contrast to dyestuff manufacturers in the countries at war, the Basel companies were not able to offset losses in their civilian business with orders from the armed forces. The economic war dampened exports, limited transport links to a few insecure routes and prevented currency exchange. However, the keenest challenge for the Basel chemical industry lay in raw material imports: most of its coal and starting products came from Germany. The Nazi regime only permitted exports within a certain framework, which had to be negotiated via the Swiss authorities responsible for the wartime economy. Geigy CEO Carl Koechlin-Vischer (1889–1969) was appointed Head of the Chemical and Pharmaceutical Industry section of the Swiss Federal Department of War, Industry and Employment. He provided the Basel chemical industry with an excellent link to the key offices of the Swiss economy in the difficult war years. Koechlin's efforts to secure the best possible provision of raw materials and German coal can hardly be overpraised. To help meet the demand for energy, coal was also mined at various sites around Switzerland. Sandoz had the Schwarzenmatt AG mine in Boltingen (Canton of Bern), from which over 6,000 tonnes of additional fuel were extracted in 1943–1944. Towards the end of the war, German deliveries of raw materials dwindled to very low levels. In this precarious situation, Basel's chemical industry focused on renovating and modernizing its production equipment.

It also expanded its research activities, because – as was noted in the 1940 Sandoz Annual Report – "only by staying ahead in terms of the quality of our products will we survive the difficult war and postwar period".

Revolutionary inventions: DDT… In the autumn of 1939, Geigy research chemist Paul Hermann Müller (1899–1965) discovered the insecticidal properties of dichlorodiphenyltrichloroethane, or DDT. As it had a broad range of applications and permanently destroyed numerous insect species, DDT quickly became the most popular insecticide. Geigy supplied the international markets with the innovative DDT products Gesarol (for agriculture) and Neocid (for control of disease-carrying insects). The company not only exported these products directly from Basel; it also had DDT manufactured at its foreign production sites and by licensed external companies. It supplied both the Axis powers and the Allies. While the US government used DDT in the war only to combat the spread of typhus and malaria, the Germans mainly employed it to protect crops. However, the unrestricted global use of DDT as a pesticide in the postwar years soon began to have worrying adverse effects: the substance got into the fat reserves of birds, mammals and humans via the food chain. After being praised initially as a miracle weapon in the fight against diseases and pests, in the 1960s DDT became the epitome of menacing toxin.

… and LSD In the 1930s, Sandoz chemist Albert Hofmann (1906–2008) resumed the company's research into ergot alkaloids begun by Arthur Stoll. Scientists at the Rockefeller Institute in New York had recently isolated the basic structural unit common to the ergot alkaloids, lysergic acid. As part of his search for a circulatory and respiratory stimulant, Hofmann synthesized various amide derivatives of lysergic acid in 1938. The 25th substance in this series was lysergic acid diethylamide, which he named LSD-25 for use in the laboratory. Pharmacological experiments with LSD-25 on animals showed that their behavior was unsettled during anaesthesia. No further effects could be ascertained. Five years later, Hofmann decided to re-examine the substance, and on April 19, 1943, he carried out his legendary self-experiment, by which he proved the psychotropic effects of this partially synthesized alkaloid. LSD-25 marked the birth of psychopharmacology, which led to the discoveries of the neurotransmitters serotonin and dopamine in the following decades. LSD research suffered a heavy setback when the psychedelic substance was caught up in the wave of recreational drug use which accompanied the hippy movement from the mid-1960s.

The immediate postwar period From an economic point of view, the war had a positive impact on Basel's chemical industry. The production facilities had not only survived the war intact, but in some cases had also been modernized, which meant they were well prepared for peacetime business. Because the Basel chemical industry was virtually the only one in Europe with fully functioning production facilities, it profited exceptionally from the economic boom of the postwar years. Products from Basel were of high quality and therefore in high demand. Only production capacities and the availability of raw materials limited sales figures. In 1951, CIBA's total sales were four times higher than in 1939.

Sandoz New York. Payroll office.
June 1944.

Sandoz San Francisco
(California, USA). Secretariat.
1944.

Sandoz Paterson (New Jersey,
USA). Laboratory. 1944.

049

**Carl Koechlin-Vischer (1889–1969).
May 17, 1968.**
Having been educated at the Basel Humanist
Grammar School, the Neuchâtel Commercial School (Switzerland) and the Berlin Com-
mercial College (Germany), Carl Koechlin
joined Geigy in 1908. After spending time in
New York, in 1914 he was named Deputy
Director and in 1918 Director. A year later he
was elected to the Board of Directors, and
was CEO from 1939. From 1949 to 1967,
he was Chairman of the Board of Directors.
Koechlin offered his services to numerous
economic organizations, including the
Swiss Federation of Trade and Industry
(now economiesuisse), the Swiss National
Bank and the Swiss Society of Chemical
Industries.

050

**The Summit site (New Jersey, USA).
August 1946.**
The CIBA subsidiary in Summit opened
in 1937 and became a leading provider in
the US pharmaceutical market during
the Second World War.

049

050

FAIRCHILD AERIAL SURVEYS INC N Y C

Sandoz Basel. Dye workers
emptying a filter press. 1950.

Sandoz Basel. Telephone
operator. 1940s.

Geigy Rio de Janeiro (Brazil).
Delivery vehicle in front
of the warehouse entrance.
1951.

051

051

**A can of Neocid and a can of Gesarol spray
from 1942.**

052

**Paul Hermann Müller (1899 – 1965) being
awarded the Nobel Prize. December 10, 1948.**
Geigy chemist Paul Müller, who discovered
the insecticidal properties of DDT, received
the Nobel Prize for Physiology or Medicine in
1948. The photo shows the Nobel Laureate
in the Concert Hall in Stockholm (Sweden)
after receiving the certificate and gold
medal.

053

**A mother in the New York borough of
Brooklyn disinfects her child's room with a
can of Neocid, also used by the US Army.
1945.**

052

Sandoz East Hanover
(New Jersey, USA). Laboratory
assistant. Between 1950
and 1952.

Geigy Basel. Color laboratory.
Early 1950s.

Geigy Schweizerhalle near Basel.
A consignment for the Red Cross.
1944.

CIBA Hong Kong. Laboratory. 1949.

054
Albert Hofmann (1906–2008, right) and his colleague W. Bischoff manufacturing the first large batches of dihydroergotamine and *Hydergin* for clinical trials. 1945.
Albert Hofmann was born in Baden (Switzerland), where he completed a commercial apprenticeship at Brown, Boveri & Cie. After passing his Matura (school-leaving exams), he studied chemistry at the University of Zurich, gaining a doctorate with distinction in 1929. From 1929 to 1971, he worked as a research chemist at Sandoz in Basel, for the last 15 years of which he headed up the department of natural products. During his research into ergot alkaloids he discovered the hallucinogenic properties of lysergic acid diethylamide (LSD) in 1943. His research led to the creation of medicines such as *Hydergin* and *Dihydergot* and the hallucinogen psilocybin. Hofmann was an honorary member of numerous associations, including the American Society of Pharmacognosy, and was awarded multiple honorary doctorates.

055
British Field Marshal Bernard Law Montgomery visits Geigy. 1950.
Montgomery's official visit to Basel included a tour of Geigy's DDT laboratories. The photo shows CEO Hartmann Koechlin-Ryhiner (1893–1962) and Paul Müller explaining an experiment cabinet (out of the photo, to the left) in which the first flies had been destroyed in 1939 using the new "miracle pesticide".

054

Sandoz Toronto (Canada).
General Secretariat. 1944.

CIBA Copenhagen (Denmark).
Commercial warehouse for
pharmaceutical products. 1948.

Sandoz Buenos Aires (Argentina).
Scientific office of Adolfo H.
Souviron. December 4, 1942.

056
Analytical balance, Sandoz East Hanover
(New Jersey, USA). Between 1950 and 1952.

057
Sandoz branch in Los Angeles (California,
USA). Around 1944.

058
The CIBA administrative building in Viale
Premuda after Milan (Italy) had suffered
heavy bombardment. August 1943.

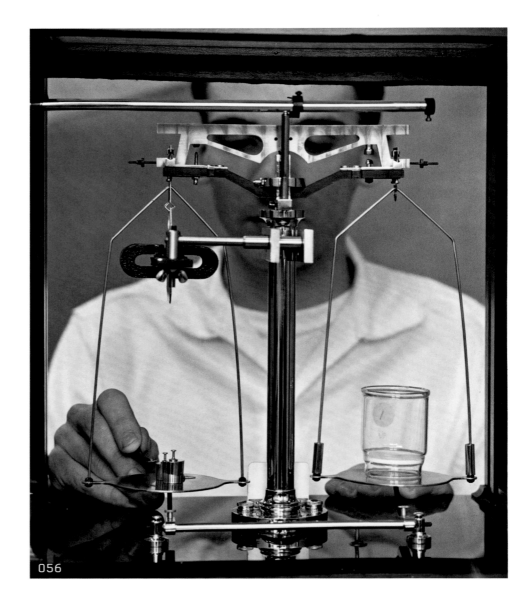

056

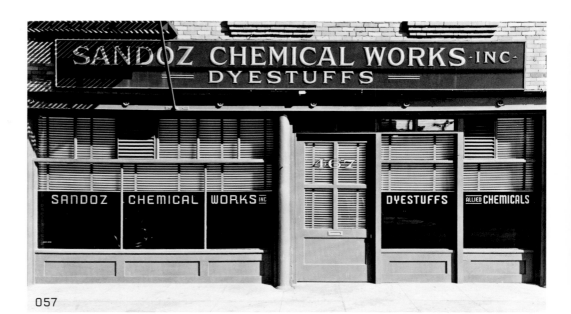

057

058

THE BATTLE AGAINST MALARIA

From cinchona bark to global partnerships

Malaria (from the Italian mala aria, "bad air") is an infectious disease spread via the bite of the Anopheles mosquito. Infected females transmit a parasite known as plasmodium, which multiplies in the liver and then attacks red blood cells. Malaria is the most common parasitic infection in the world (in 2019 there were an estimated 229 million cases of malaria) and occurs primarily in the poorest countries. Without treatment, malaria leads among other things to circulatory problems, which can be fatal.

A predecessor company of Novartis first dealt with malaria in the 1810s. Among the colonial products sold by Hieronymus Geigy (1771–1830) was cinchona, which had been known to be effective against malaria since the 17th century. Originally from South America, this remedy was used to treat "stomach illnesses and fever". In 1824, quinine was isolated from cinchona. The Geigy company was among the first buyers of this new pure substance, whose advantage was that it enabled standardized treatment and more precise dosage for malaria patients.

A number of measures have been taken with the aim of reducing cases and indeed epidemics of malaria. One such measure was the draining of marshland, which provides the breeding ground for many types of mosquito. Another key milestone in the battle against malaria was the discovery of the insecticidal effect of DDT (dichlorodiphenyltrichloroethane), whose industrial production began at Geigy during the Second World War. Use of this product wiped out malaria in the USA, Canada and Europe in particular. A highly impressive example here is Italy: in 1946, almost 300,000 people died of malaria there; by 1950 there was not one fatality.

DDT was banned in the 1970s due to environmental concerns. Later, the World Health Organization (WHO) reassessed DDT and ultimately, in 2006, authorized restricted use of the product inside buildings in order to reduce the number of infections in regions where malaria reaches epidemic proportions. The development of resistance in Anopheles mosquitoes and malaria parasites, however, is hampering the treatment and eradication of this disease. In some cases, malaria therapies have become ineffective. For this reason, improving those is a top priority.

Novartis achieved an important innovation here with the launch of *Coartem* in 1999. The active substances in this drug are lumefantrine, a molecule which is effective against malaria, and artemether. Artemether is a derivative of artemisinin, which is isolated from artemisia, a plant very well known in Chinese medicine. The components of *Coartem* are not related to quinine, meaning that they are also effective against chloroquine-resistant malaria pathogens. The traditional malaria drug chloroquine had lost more than 50 per cent of its efficacy. For this reason, the WHO recommended a combination therapy using artemisinin derivates as first-line treatment for malaria.

In 2001, a not-for profit partnership with the WHO was unveiled – the "Novartis Malaria Initiative". Novartis undertook to supply the WHO with Coartem at cost price. As a result, authorities in 60 of the world's poorest

1
Artemisia planter. 2012.
Novartis worked with around 100,000 farmers in China who grow *Artemisia annua*.

2
A Greek building after treatment with DDT. 1946.

1

2

Raising awareness of malaria. 2011.
A teacher in a Kenyan village school
familiarizes the children with the prevention
and correct treatment of malaria.

countries received nearly 900 million treatments. Meanwhile, entirely new challenges are emerging. Increasing resistance in patients against artemisinin and other currently employed malaria treatments is manifesting itself. In 2018, therefore, Novartis announced the investment of 100 million US dollars in the research and development of new medicines in the coming five years.

3

6 TWO DECADES OF GROWTH

GLOBAL EXPANSION AND A MARRIAGE
1950–1970

The economies of the West grew by leaps and bounds in the 1950s and 1960s. This ongoing boom brought about a phenomenal increase in the sales of the Basel chemical companies, with figures soaring from millions of Swiss francs into the billions. The Basel companies set up a network of sales channels, production sites and research centers around the globe and gained a foothold in new business sectors.

Sandoz on a global expansion course Sandoz is a striking example of the globalization of the Basel companies in the middle of the century. After the end of the Second World War, Sandoz set up companies one by one in India, Ireland, Mexico, the Netherlands, Portugal, Canada, Venezuela, Sweden, Argentina and Uruguay. In 1956, the group had 19 subsidiaries abroad. By 1966, the number of foreign subsidiaries had risen to almost 40, and included Australia, Cuba, New Zealand, Japan, Morocco, Chile, Peru, Colombia, Pakistan, the Philippines and Finland. Sandoz did not follow longterm or even medium-term strategies in these new markets: in the general economic upswing, everything was more or less improvised. In 1963, a pharmaceutical distribution department was set up which encompassed marketing consultancy, market research, product management, specialist medical consultancy, planning, journals, translation and four country units. This structure was designed to ensure more intensive management of markets and products.

Pharmaceuticals become a boom business The quarter century following the end of the war was a phase of enormous growth for the pharmaceutical industry in all western industrial nations. The Pharmaceuticals Divisions of CIBA and Sandoz became their strongest business segments. Between 1945 and 1960, CIBA increased its sales in this area from around 100 million Swiss francs to over 500 million. These high growth rates can be attributed to various factors: on the demand side, rising prosperity and the expansion of the health insurance sector were crucial. In the USA, the most important sales market for medicines, the number of people insured increased ten-fold between 1940 and 1960, from just over 12 million to more than 120 million. On the supply side, increasing public and private research investment boosted the rate of innovation throughout the sector. From the late 1940s onwards, the number of medicines launched each year rose considerably. The industry introduced a broad spectrum of new antibiotics, allergy medications, sedatives, chemotherapy agents, cardiovascular medicines, psychotropics, analgesics, steroid hormones and vitamin products to the market.

Production is decentralized In the 1950s and 1960s, the booming Basel chemical industry greatly expanded its production base in Switzerland and abroad. Two objectives lay behind these investments in the pharmaceutical business: first, the few existing chemical factories were to be upgraded, as they were having to produce ever-increasing quantities of active substances. Second, the pharmaceutical sector needed to have a large number of production facilities around the world in order to supply local markets. Another reason for building new production sites abroad was that more and more countries – especially the non-industrialized ones – had introduced customs duties, exchange regulations and import licenses with the aim of ensuring that, if possible, everything from the active substance through to the finished product would be produced in their own country.

Research and development move abroad The Basel chemical industry had been internationally active in sales and production for some time, and now it also began to cross national borders in its research and development work. From the 1950s onwards, CIBA massively expanded its US research and development activities in Summit (New Jersey, USA). In India, it opened a basic research center for dyestuffs and pharmaceuticals in Goregaon near Mumbai in 1963. In late 1959, Geigy purchased a laboratory building for organic chemistry, biochemistry and pharmacology in Ardsley (New York). This step enabled the company to pursue its own pharmaceutical research in the USA. Sandoz followed suit five years later, building a pharmaceutical research center in East Hanover (New Jersey, USA) in 1964. 1970 saw the inauguration of the Sandoz Research Institute in Vienna (Austria).

New diversifications open up new markets At the end of the 1950s, CIBA entered the photochemistry, electronic equipment and animal health sectors. Sandoz acquired the Austrian company Biochemie GmbH in Kundl in 1963, thereby gaining a foothold in the antibiotics and biotechnology sector. In 1967, Sandoz laid the foundations of its nutrition business when it merged with Wander in Bern (Switzerland). This merger also expanded its own pharmaceutical range and allowed it to take over a broad, well-established international distribution organization. Out of necessity rather than voluntarily, the company also entered the hospital supply sector, as a Canadian subsidiary of Wander also joined Sandoz as part of the merger. With annual sales of some 40 million Swiss francs in the hospital supply business, this subsidiary was making almost zero profit. Sandoz acquired numerous smaller firms from 1969, thereby rapidly expanding the new segment.

Sandoz expands its headquarters In 1940, the three partners in Basler IG had together secured a majority holding in the long-standing company Durand & Huguenin. The new owners did not want to strengthen a competitor further, so Durand & Huguenin continued to restrict its activities to the dyestuffs business. As that sector continued to decline, the company had few prospects for the future and was integrated into neighboring Sandoz in 1969. As a result, Sandoz gained an extra area of some 29,000 square meters, a useful addition to the Basel site.

The "Basel marriage": CIBA and Geigy merge Both CIBA and Sandoz were expanding thanks to their pharmaceutical business. The spectacular rates of growth recorded by Geigy, however, were all due to its highly successful agrochemicals, which achieved terrific sales, especially in the USA. Between 1956 and 1966, group sales had risen from 511 million Swiss francs to almost 2 billion Swiss francs. In 1967, the company caught up with CIBA in terms of sales, and figures surged to 2.7 billion Swiss francs in 1968. At the Board of Directors meeting of March 28, 1969, Geigy Chairman Louis von Planta acknowledged the excellent fiscal year and forecast a further upturn in the near future. However, the coming years would also bring enormous challenges, he said. "In this respect," von Planta warned, "we are facing two dangers: the enormous cost explosion, in particular in the research sector, and growing pressure from competitors, not only from the large German, British and American chemical companies, but also from the oil industry, which has access to virtually unlimited resources. The problem for the Board of Directors and the Executive Committee is this: how can we guarantee the growth that is essential to survive in such a competitive environment?" Von Planta saw the solution in a closer collaboration with another Basel company. Sandoz had signaled "a certain willingness to enter into a precisely defined collaboration in specific areas, but not an all-encompassing cooperation agreement". CIBA, on the other hand, had indicated "spontaneous willingness to enter into an extremely wide-ranging collaboration". Two weeks later, the Boards of CIBA and Geigy announced that they were looking into a possible merger of their companies in more detail. On October 20, 1970, shareholders in the two companies approved the merger agreement at respective extraordinary general meetings.

Some criticism was voiced before the merger, however, in particular on the Geigy side. On April 5, 1969, Geigy Board member Johann Jakob Vischer (1914–1985) wrote to von Planta. He emphasized that Geigy had developed a management style which gave it an edge over other companies and "of which we are all a little proud. It would be a great pity if that were to be lost." The collaboration did indeed prove to be difficult, as the two companies had developed completely different cultures. For a long time, the newly merged Ciba-Geigy workforce remained loyal to either the former Geigy or to the former CIBA – including all of their practices, cliques, procedures and products.

The foundation of the Friedrich Miescher Institute (FMI) During the merger negotiations with Geigy, CIBA decided to set up an institute for basic research in the field of biology. This was partly as a reaction to a local competitor who had taken a similar step: in 1967, Roche had founded an institute for basic biomedical research in the USA, and had set up another in Switzerland just one year later. This caused a certain amount of anxiety among the other three Basel chemical companies. On April 10, 1970, CIBA and Geigy signed a charter describing the tasks of the institute, which was named after the Basel-based physician and physiologist Friedrich Miescher, the man who discovered nucleic acid. These tasks included training young scientists and conducting basic biomedical research. Right from the start, the FMI placed great emphasis on acting out its role as a bridge between universities and industry, something which the Roche institutes took upon themselves too.

Geigy Porto (Portugal). Experimental dyeworks. Between 1952 and 1953.

Sandoz Mexico City. Canteen. 1952.

CIBA Horsham (UK). Tube filling in Building 12. May 1953.

S.A. Española de Colorantes Sintéticos in Hospitalet near Barcelona (Spain), a Sandoz holding. Laboratory. Probably 1964.

CIBA Wehr (Germany). Dyeworks. 1960s.

059
Headquarters of Sandoz de México S.A. in Mexico City. June 6, 1952.

060
Laboratory at the CIBA site in Stein (Switzerland). Around 1960.
CIBA built a new pharmaceutical production site in Stein in 1957. It went on to become the company's most important pharmaceutical factory.

060

Geigy Rio de Janeiro (Brazil).
Entrance to the pharmaceutical
department on the 6th floor
of the Edifício Mayapan.
Around 1953.

Geigy Rio de Janeiro. An employee
filling pesticide. 1956.

CIBA Copenhagen (Denmark).
Analytical pharmaceutical
laboratory. 1960s.

CIBA Copenhagen. Goods
dispatch. 1960s.

CIBA Copenhagen. Invoicing.
1960s.

061
Opening of the CIBA Research Center in Goregaon near Mumbai (India). March 21, 1963.
Indian Prime Minister Jawaharlal Nehru opened the new research center established by CIBA and described this investment in his speech as a valuable contribution to the establishment of science and industry in India.

062 | 063
Geigy Chemical Corporation Inc., Ardsley (New York). 1956.
In 1956, Geigy USA moved from the old-fashioned Barclay Street in New York to the ultramodern buildings of its new head office in Ardsley. Since the entire building complex had been redesigned and constructed from scratch, every department was able to have specific rooms tailored to its needs.

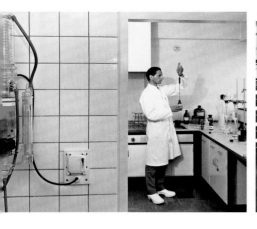

Sandoz Basel. Color laboratory.
November 1957.

Sandoz Basel. Crystallization of
cardiac glycosides in Building 316.
1956.

Sandoz Basel. Enjoying a break
on the roof of the packaging
factory (Building 310). Probably
1959.

Sandoz Nuremberg (Germany).
Ampoule station. 1960.

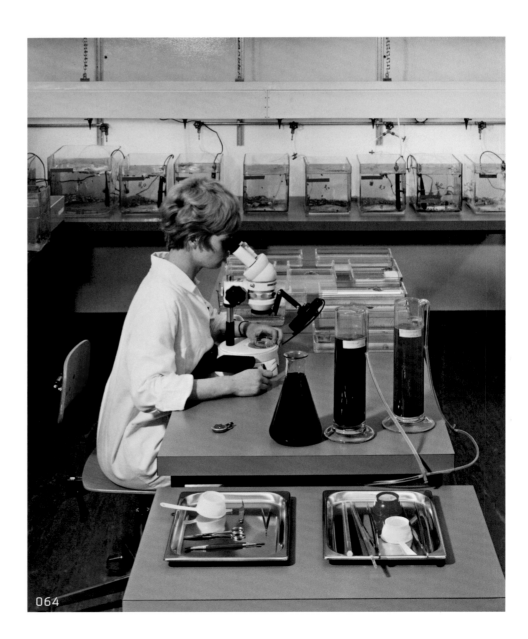

064
**Parasitology laboratory (snail breeding)
at the Sandoz Research Institute in Vienna
(Austria). Early 1970s.**

065
**Electron beam recorder at the Ilford
processing plant in Basildon (UK). 1970.**
In 1969, CIBA acquired the remaining share
capital in the British photographic company
Ilford, having owned a holding in the
company since 1966.

065

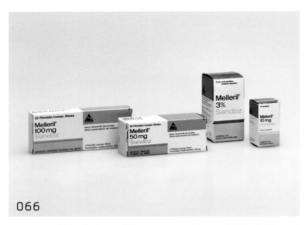

066

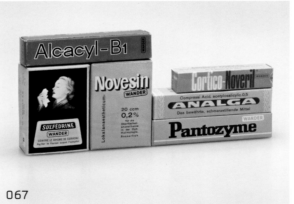

067

068

066
Melleril packaging. 1980s.
Sandoz launched the neuroleptic *Melleril* in 1958. This new medicine was highly effective for a wide range of psychoses and was well tolerated. *Melleril* gained acceptance in clinical and outpatient psychiatric treatment as an efficient sedative for a broad spectrum of indications. In the 1960s and 1970s, it made a major contribution to the sales of the Sandoz Pharmaceuticals Division. In 1980, it was still the primary neuroleptic on the global market.

067
Pharmaceutical products from Wander. Between 1940 and 1970.
The Swiss industrial company Wander AG from Bern manufactured special foodstuffs (dietetics, in particular malt products, sports and infant nutrition and slimming products) and pharmaceuticals focused on the areas of pain relief, colds, gastrointestinal disorders, skin diseases, rheumatic disorders and psychiatry.

068
Ovaltine/Ovomaltine range. 1991.
The best-known and strongest-selling product in the Wander nutrition business was the malt drink Ovaltine/Ovomaltine, which was launched in 1904.

069
Fermenter systems for performing microbiological processes at Sandoz in Kundl (Austria). Probably 1966.

069

Geigy Basel. Checking the color
shades of carpet wool. 1965.

Geigy Basel. Pest control
research. 1966.

070

**Printed menu "Lunch d'adieu .. à CIBA –
(Ré) action de collaborateurs – 19 octobre
1970". October 1970.**

071

Louis Fortunat von Planta (1917–2003). 1974.
Louis von Planta attended the Basel Humanist Grammar School and went on to study law
at the University of Basel. In 1939, he took
his doctoral and bar exams. He was a partner
at a Basel lawyer's and notary's office
from 1946 to 1967. In 1965, he was elected to
the Geigy Board of Directors, becoming its
Chairman in 1968. He acted as a driving force
behind the merger of CIBA and Geigy.
From 1972 to 1987, he was Chairman and CEO
of Ciba-Geigy, and became Honorary Chairman
after that. In 1973, he was awarded an
honorary doctorate by the University
of Fribourg (Switzerland) and, in 1986, the
Friendship Prize of the American-Swiss
Association. As Chairman of the Swiss
Federation of Trade and Industry (now
economiesuisse) from 1976 to 1987, Louis von
Planta gave lasting service to the Swiss
economy. Thanks to his wealth of experience
and contacts, he made a vital contribution
to preparing the merger of Ciba and Sandoz
to form Novartis. From 1996 to 2003,
he was Honorary Chairman of Novartis.

072

Robert Käppeli (1900–2000). 1948.
Robert Käppeli was born in Lucerne (Switzerland). After completing his commercial
training, he studied macroeconomics in Basel,
earning a doctorate in 1928. He then worked
as an assistant at the Institute for the
World Economy and Maritime Traffic in Kiel
(Germany) and as Secretary to the directors
of the Warburg Bank in Hamburg (Germany).
He joined CIBA as secretary to the Board
of Directors in 1934, becoming head of the
finance department in 1939 and CEO in 1946.
In 1956, he was promoted to Chairman of
the CIBA Board of Directors. Käppeli was the
first Chairman of Ciba-Geigy from 1970 to 1972,
then Honorary Chairman of the Board and,
from 1996, Honorary Chairman of Novartis.
He was a member of several boards of
directors and various art committees. He was
awarded honorary doctorates by the Federal
Institute of Technology in Zurich and the Swiss
universities of Fribourg and Basel.

MENU

Lunch d'adieu . . à CIBA
— (Ré) action de collaborateurs —
19 octobre 1970

Pâté Grands Chasseurs
Sauce "alliance"

"Structured" Roast Beef a la mode de CI-GEI-NER
Sauce "Intégration" au goût des patrons –, adaptée à
toutes "fonctions"

Pommes sautées à point . . de "fusion"

Légumes de fin de saison relevés
d'"Additifs" parfumés

Salade de "divisions" aux pi(g)ments "régionaux"

Les fromages de qualité:
Crème Petite Chapelle
Vacherin – Veau d'or
Be – LY – paese

"pain" pour le prochain qualité VICTORIA

Fruits assortis de nos propres PLANTA-tions
Pâtisserie à discrétion en tranches de "participation"

Café et liqueurs "diversifiées"
articles de "Grande Consommation"

Vins 1ers crus

millésimes garantis antérieurs à 1969
mis en bouteilles en usines
"dépôt à l'exportation" assuré

Cigares réconfortants qualité Fidel

070

071

072

CIBA Osaka (Japan).
Packing *Ritalin*. Probably 1962.

CIBA Origgio (Italy).
Dyestuff laboratory. 1964.

CIBA Origgio. Dyestuff laboratory.
1965.

073

074

073
Ritalin packaging. 1960s.
Methylphenidate, a substance synthesized in the research laboratories at CIBA in 1944, was launched in 1954 as a stimulant under the trade name of *Ritalin*. Contemporary product information recommended the drug "for increased fatigability, lack of concentration, memory lapses with insufficient coordination and association ability (arteriosclerosis), depressive moods (e.g. reactive climacteric or convalescent depression), avolition and narcolepsy".

074
CIBA Lisbon (Portugal). Administration building constructed in 1961. January 1964.

075
Origgio. Office building. 1964.
In 1965, CIBA moved its head office in Italy from Milan to the nearby town of Origgio. The new buildings were built according to the very latest latest architectural and functional criteria.

076
Origgio. Open-plan office. 1965.
Origgio had open-plan offices. To reduce noise to a minimum, sound-absorbing material was used for the ceilings, the floors were covered with wall-to-wall carpets and all metal furniture was removed, as were typewriters and calculators that did not function quietly enough. Furthermore, the individual working groups were separated by half-height cupboards and numerous plants.

075

076

CIBA Basel. Building 147,
reading room in the library
(E. Meier, Dr. R. Neher,
Dr. B. Schär, Dr. F. Kahnt).
Around 1960.

CIBA Basel. Building 147,
post room (A. Fichter,
E. Eichenberger). Around 1960.

CIBA Basel. Building 147, film
room (H. Walz). Around 1960.

077

**Time-Sharing Computer Center of Sandoz
AG, Basel. October or November 1969.**
Swiss companies were early users of computer technology, usually known then as
electronic data processing (EDP). This gained
traction from the 1960s, being employed in
the commercial-administrative as well as the
technical-scientific areas. In 1967, Sandoz
purchased a UNIVAC-1108 system from the
Sperry Rand company, and this was installed
in the new administrative tower block in the
spring of 1968. A myriad of peripheral devices
was attached to this mainframe computer.
As a forerunner of the modern hard disk,
it had drum storage of various capacities.
Via telephone lines, the communications
subsystem was connected to a large number
of input and output devices for remote data
processing in offices, laboratories and ware-
houses.

078

**Renovation of Tower Bridge in London using
rapidly hardening epoxy resin adhesive from
CIBA. 1962.**
Epoxy resins were developed in the 1930s.
CIBA was the first company to manufacture
this synthetic resin class on an industrial
scale and brought it to market under the
name Araldite in 1946. Ten years later, there
were more than 30 product variations of the
adhesive. They were used in the electrical
industry, construction, vehicle manufacture,
air and space travel as well as the restora-
tion of antiquities (e.g. in bonding or stabi-
lization of the porous stone of the relocated
Egyptian temple complex Abu Simbel).

077

Geigy Basel. Laboratory technician
training facility. 1961.

Geigy Basel. Shorthand typists.
Probably 1962.

Sandoz Basel. Kitchen in staff
restaurant. 1965.

079

**Sound movie projector above the driver's
seat in the Geigy Cinema Truck. 1953.**
As early as the 1910s, industrial films were
employed as a means of company communication. This applied to the consumer goods,
watch and clock, electrical, engineering and
vehicle industries. They were promotional,
manufacturing or training films. However,
it was the Swiss national exhibition of 1939
in Zurich that galvanized the chemicals
sector into setting up films. From 1945, Geigy
used mainly advertising films for pesticides,
aiming them at farmers and housewives.
To make personal contact with customers,
from March 1953 Geigy employees travelled
around north-west and north-east Switzerland with an exhibition and a cinema truck.
This on-the-road cinema was equipped with
a sound movie projector above the driver's
seat. The rear wall served as projection
screen for the 30 seats available. Demon-
stration films about pest control in houses
and gardens as well as in farms were shown.

080

CIBA Dorval (Canada). Canteen. 1960s.

079

080

GEIGY DESIGN

Good design for good business

1
Portfolio for Documenta Geigy/Animales dormidos ("sleeping animals"). Gottfried Honegger. 1955.

2
Advertising card for the antipruritic Eurax. Andreas His. 1956.

3
Envelope for the company newspaper "Geigy Catalyst" no. 16. Fred Troller. 1964.

The dynamic growth of Geigy led to the foundation of a group-wide "publicity department" in 1941, which was renamed as the advertising department in 1966. The turning point was the launch campaign for the industrial moth-proofing agent Mitin in 1939. For the first time in its history, the company – which had specialized in dyestuffs until the 1920s – was faced with the challenge of appealing not just to industrial customers but also to private households. An agency was commissioned, but the advertising slogan it came up with failed to hit the mark with the public. This unsuccessful campaign prompted the conclusion that the company needed its own advertising specialists, and the emergence of intensively marketed Geigy pharmaceutical products made a central publicity department seem absolutely essential. The job of setting up this department was entrusted to René Rudin (1911–1992), who managed it until 1970. His advertising policy was based on five principles, which he outlined in 1944:

1. Our publicity must maintain a factual tone for all products.
2. To ensure the necessary penetration, we must employ suitable suggestive elements, tailored carefully to the consumer group being targeted.
3. We must ensure that certain artistic standards are maintained, by means of immaculate typographical design, high quality image material and flawless reproduction in printed form.
4. All printed material leaving our company and all our other statements must express the trustworthiness of the name Geigy, thereby functioning as goodwill publicity above and beyond their immediate purpose.
5. We must strive to give our publicity its own special character, with the goal of gradually creating a typical Geigy style.

To avoid the danger that internal advertising experts (in contrast to external agencies) would sooner or later fall into a routine and become blinkered, Rudin always kept things fresh in his department: his team employed young, talented graphic artists, designers, editors and filmmakers, and also used the services of freelance photographers and artists for certain tasks. The studio at the firm's headquarters maintained close ties with the Basel General Vocational School in particular, promoting a lively exchange between design training and practice. This was an important factor in turning Basel into a pool of talent which helped spread Swiss graphic design around the world and give it international recognition.

The development and quality of graphics and advertising at Geigy resulted mainly from astute HR policies, and not from prescribed design guidelines. In the three decades from 1941 to 1970, over 50 designers were employed internally or as freelancers at the Basel headquarters. A further two dozen or so worked primarily in the 1960s for the studios of subsidiaries in the USA and the UK, as well as in Spain, Italy, Canada and Australia, although these countries only had small advertising teams.

"Solutions which make the abstract concrete and understandable." That was how the specialist publication of 1967, *Chemie, Werbung und Grafik* ("Chemistry, Advertising and Graphic Design"), defined the core task of pro-

2

Documenta Geigy

Animales dormidos

1

3

4
Envelope for an Irgapyrine brochure
(against inflammatory irritations of the eye).
Igildo Biesele. 1953–1956.

5
Blotting board (promotional gift for
physicians) for the anti-fungal *Sterosan*.
Nelly Rudin. 1952.

6
Insert for process yellow 4GL.
Toshihiro Katayama. 1963–1964.

moting chemical and pharmaceutical achievements. Medicines for a broad range of indications, textile care products and pesticides differ at most in terms of their form; our senses do not directly perceive their effect. Their benefit is an abstract concept for the consumer and using them requires a great deal of trust, which is derived from the manufacturer's image.

These specific circumstances unlocked extraordinary design potential among the Geigy graphic artists of the 1950s and early 1960s. In most cases, it was expressed in a distinctly modern formal language which does not seem schematic or formulaic but remains fresh, flexible and individual. As a result, design personalities such as Max Schmid, Karl Gerstner, Gottfried Honegger, Nelly Rudin, Roland Aeschlimann and Toshihiro Katayama created a corporate diversity that provided a platform for pictorial symbolism and incisive typography and also for lessons in non-representational art. The designs, which were soon referred to as being in the "Geigy style", are characterized by reduction to a few elements, generous use of white space, equal use of graphics and photography, strong lines, stark contrasts between dark, light and color, geometric construction, unusual materials and processing techniques, and the almost exclusive use of sans serif fonts.

Geigy's industrial design was soon looked upon as a new benchmark: in 1967, Princeton University began an exhibition series on modern graphic design. The first show was entitled "Geigy Graphics" and primarily presented works by Geigy USA under Fred Troller.

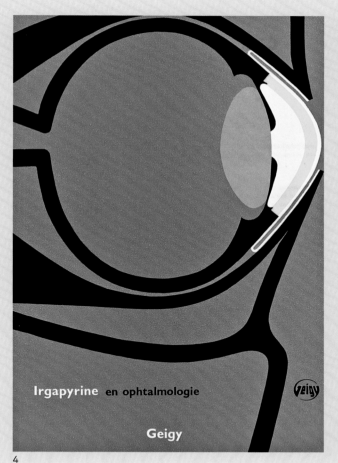

Irgapyrine en ophtalmologie

Geigy

4

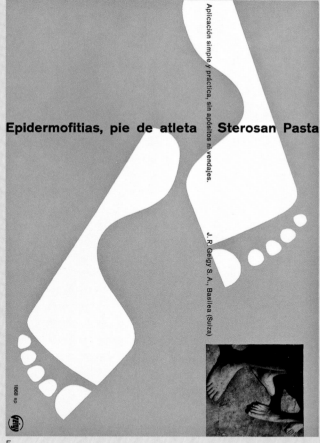

Aplicación simple y práctica, sin apósitos ni vendajes.

Epidermofitias, pie de atleta Sterosan Pasta

J. R. Geigy S. A., Basilea (Suiza)

1868 sp

5

Das Papier, deutsch/Deutschland, 210×297, 6000   Alleinhersteller: J. R. Geigy A.G., Basel, Schweiz

GEIGY

Ein brillantes grünstichiges Direktgelb

Papierechtgelb 4GL für sämtliche gebleichten Sorten

J. R. Geigy A.G., Basel, Schweiz   Geigy Verkaufsgesellschaft m.b.H., Frankfurt am Main, Liebigstraße 51/53
«Gerola» Warenhandelsgesellschaft m.b.H., Bregenz, Römerstraße 1; Wien 1, Stubenring 24

6

TOFRANIL

A revolution in treating depression

The research on psychological changes carried out in the 1930s only bore fruit after the Second World War. In 1952, surgeon Henri Laborit discovered by chance that the molecule chlorpromazine alleviates shock caused by surgery and improves the mood of postoperative patients. Consequently, psychiatrists began to use chlorpromazine to treat unsettled patients. It was the first in the class of medicines known as neuroleptics, and enabled use of the straitjacket – which was customary at the time – to be avoided. Geigy, too, was involved in researching the efficacy of chlorpromazine. In 1953, Swiss psychiatrist Roland Kuhn asked Geigy to provide him with psychotropic substances to treat his schizophrenia patients at the Münsterlingen Cantonal Hospital (Switzerland). He was given samples of imipramine, a compound which had a tricyclic structure similar to that of chlorpromazine and which had been described by the Geigy pharmacologists. Kuhn tested the substance for two years and ascertained that it did not have the expected neuroleptic effect. After treatment of 150 patients, however, an antidepressive effect became apparent. In September 1957, Kuhn presented the findings of his clinical tests at the second World Congress of Psychiatry in Zurich. One year later, imipramine, under the name *Tofranil*, became the first antidepressant to be launched. It was soon established globally as a well-tolerated standard treatment for endogenous depression or melancholia, and triggered a genuine revolution in psychiatry. Before the launch of *Tofranil*, depression patients had to spend long periods in clinics and were often treated with electroshock therapy, as the only options were to stimulate or sedate them; it was impossible to restore their overall equilibrium and normalize their mood. With an efficacy rate of over 80 per cent, *Tofranil* was, for a long time, the gold standard in treatment of all types of depression, allowing a significant reduction in the number of inpatient treatments.

Based on these experiences, further research by Geigy led to the discovery of another substance with significant potential: chlorimipramine. It was presented to psychiatrists at a congress in 1961, and met with great acclaim. After five-year trials in renowned clinics, the new tricyclic was brought onto the market in 1966 under the name *Anafranil*. In addition to depression, this medicine is used to treat conditions such as obsessive-compulsive disorder, panic attacks, agoraphobia, certain types of bed-wetting in children and neuropathic pain. *Anafranil* has proved to be an extremely effective medicine which brings about high remission rates.

In 1972, Ciba-Geigy launched the product *Ludiomil*. It contained a new substance called maprotiline, a tetracyclic indicated for treating various types of depression. It helps to restore high-quality sleep and reduces anxiety, although it is not employed specifically in the treatment of panic attacks. In the last 50 years, the therapeutic spectrum of depression treatment has widened significantly, but tri- and tetracyclics (although they are prescribed less often than in the past) remain a reliable alternative.

1–4
Watercolors by draughtsman and illustrator Tomi Ungerer on the topic of depression. 1972. © Tomi Ungerer/Diogenes Verlag AG, Zurich.

1

2

HELPLESSNESS

3

4

VOLTAREN

A classic treatment for
rheumatism and pain

Rheumatism comes in many different forms. This chronic disease, still incurable, involves a large number of painful inflammatory disorders of the joints, vertebrae, muscles, tendons and connective tissue.

Rheumatic symptoms were described as early as the 5th century BC by Greek physician and scholar Hippocrates of Kos. In those days, the juice of willow bark (*Salix* species) was the treatment of choice. The first medicines for rheumatic complaints were only created at the end of the 19th century, however. In 1828, the willow bark extract salicin was isolated, which the body metabolizes into biologically active salicylic acid. From 1874, this substance was manufactured industrially in Germany at Dr. F. von Heyden's salicylic acid factories in Dresden and Radebeul and sold as a medicine. Owing to its side effects and bitter taste, further research was carried out. In 1897, the main Bayer factory in Elberfeld (now Wuppertal, Germany) managed to produce the structurally related acetylsalicylic acid – first synthesized by Charles Frédéric Gerhardt in 1853 – in pure form. Bayer called the product Aspirin and had it patented in 1899. Acetylsalicylic acid turned out to be very useful for therapeutic purposes. However, in the 20th century, new substances with superior analgesic and anti-inflammatory properties emerged.

From 1953 to 1964, Geigy led the market for antirheumatics with its product *Butazolidin* (from phenylbutazone, which was discovered in 1946). When US pharmaceutical group Merck presented the one hundred times more active indomethacin in 1964, Geigy began the search for a new, highly active and well-tolerated anti-inflammatory. First, Geigy chemists compared known non-steroidal antirheumatics. Due to remarkable physico-chemical similarities, it was possible to define crucial basic structural requirements for a new substance. When, during the development phase in 1966, this drug proved to be poorly tolerated by rats and dogs – as had also been the case with clinically active indomethacin – the group leader decided to try it out on himself. A two-day trial of the new active substance diclofenac caused no complications and encouraged Geigy to push ahead with its development. Tolerability studies in healthy volunteers and the subsequent clinical trial confirmed the substance's activity and tolerability. Ciba-Geigy launched the product in Japan and Switzerland under the brand name *Voltaren* in 1974. Since then, it has become established in over 140 countries as a reliable medication for all forms of rheumatism and numerous conditions involving acute pain and inflammation. With 200,000 participants in clinical trials and over a billion patients treated, it is one of the best-studied medicines in the world. Its numerous dosages and dosage forms (including ampoules, eye drops, emulsion gels, patches, tablets and suppositories) ensure individually tailored medical care and contribute to the product's continuing popularity.

1
Title page of a specialist *Voltaren* brochure for Austria. December 1976.

2
Some of the many dosage forms of *Voltaren* over the years: sugar-coated tablets, ampoules and emulsion gel from Geigy, and emulsion gel, slow-release sugar-coated tablets and eye drops (*Voltaren Ophtha*) from Novartis.

1

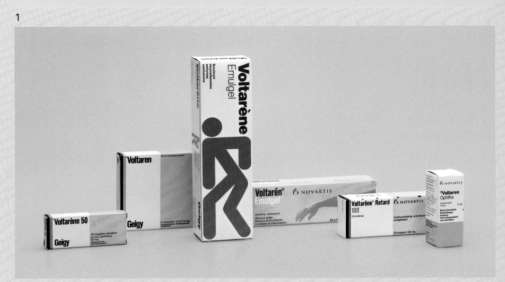

2

131

7 FIRST ONE MERGER, THEN ANOTHER

FOCUS INSTEAD OF DIVERSIFICATION
1970–1996

The 1973 oil crisis brought the longstanding economic boom in the western industrialized nations to an end. What followed was recession, inflation and currency turmoil. A new wave of globalization set in around 1980, which intensified in the 1990s. Companies striving for profitable growth were forced to set clear priorities and maintain a consistent international focus.

Diversification – the magic formula of the 1970s In the recession of the 1970s, both Ciba-Geigy and Sandoz sought new ways of spreading risks rationally. The two companies examined numerous diversification options. In 1971, Sandoz entered the fitness business, acquiring a majority stake in John Valentine. The Executive Committee saw in this project "the only immediately realizable diversification opportunity" for the pharmaceutical department, but the undertaking failed and was dropped a few years later. In 1974, Ciba-Geigy acquired Airwick Industries in Carlstadt (New Jersey, USA), a manufacturer of air fresheners, disinfectants and cleaning agents for households and large-scale consumers as well as of chemicals for swimming pools. In 1974, Ciba-Geigy entered the seeds business, a move followed by Sandoz in 1975.

The recession of the 1970s: a slump in the industrial divisions The pharmaceutical business proved to be largely resistant to economic fluctuations. Ciba-Geigy and Sandoz survived the recessions of the 1970s relatively unscathed. The oil crisis did not hit the corporations as a whole particularly hard, although energy costs did rise considerably. Only the industrial divisions – dyestuffs, chemicals, plastics, additives and pigments – faced serious problems with the supply of raw materials. The strength of the Swiss franc also took its toll on business: between 1973 and October 1978, the US$ exchange rate fell from 4.375 Swiss francs to 1.45 Swiss francs. Within the companies, it was the industrial divisions which suffered the worst dip in sales and profits as a result of the recession, a development which, over the long term, sealed their decline in the group hierarchies.

Sandoz cuts personnel costs: the overhead value analysis The economic environment changed radically in the 1970s. Sandoz's return on equity fell by more than half over the course of the decade. The results of this downward trend were particularly apparent at head office, which housed key research and production departments as well as various functions of the group headquarters. In 1976, personnel costs stood at 32 per cent of head office revenue, but by 1980 this figure had risen to 36.6 per cent. Sandoz was the first large European company to decide to reduce its administrative expenditure long-term. Consultancy firm McKinsey carried out an overhead value analysis at the Basel headquarters in 1981, with the aim of identifying weak points in the business in order to increase productivity and efficiency. All key functions and work processes were placed under critical scrutiny. The results showed that the departments examined could reduce their personnel by more than 15 per cent without weakening the company's performance. This generated considerable cost savings, with staff numbers being reduced primarily by means of natural attrition and early retirements. The resources this released were then used for targeted acquisitions, which boosted Sandoz's ability to compete.

Diversifications in the 1980s In 1980, Ciba-Geigy group management began to restructure in two directions. Firstly, it cut back activities with few prospects of generating a profit in the long term. Secondly, it sought out and entered new, lucrative areas for investment such as the precision balances and contact lens sectors, rapidly expanding both areas in the years that followed. Sandoz took over a US and a Japanese company in the construction chemicals sector in 1985, before acquiring a US environmental technology company in 1988. One year later, Sandoz combined the construction chemicals and environmental technology sectors into an independent division under the company name MBT Holding.

The Schweizerhalle blaze In the early hours of November 1, 1986, there was a fire in a warehouse at the Sandoz site in Schweizerhalle near Basel. A disaster alert was sounded in the Basel region – the population was in shock. The water used to fight the fire washed tonnes of pollutants, mainly insecticides, into the Rhine, causing environmental damage as far downstream as the Netherlands. According to the official inquiry, the fire had been caused by glowing particles of the chemical Prussian blue. The blaze at the Schweizerhalle site undermined belief in the safety of the chemical industry. It happened just a few months after the devastating nuclear disaster in Chernobyl (Ukraine) and destroyed the myth that such technology-related catastrophes were impossible in Switzerland.

The chemical industry, the authorities and politicians all drew important lessons from the Schweizerhalle blaze. The chemical industry optimized its risk reduction measures. Legal regulations and checks were tightened, and the chemical and biological monitoring of water quality intensified. Sandoz also set up the "Rhine Fund", which financed 36 scientific projects on the Rhine ecosystem. An overall evaluation shows that the water quality and the biological condition of the Rhine as a whole have improved considerably in the years since the disaster.

Biotechnology: external knowledge for internal research The first biotechnology companies began emerging in the USA in the mid-1970s; shortly afterwards, they were springing up like mushrooms. This was a result of considerable advances in molecular genetics and the interest of venture capital firms in new opportunities. Another boost for these new companies was the change in the legal framework in 1980, when the US Supreme Court authorized the patenting of genetically modified organisms. Numerous pending patent applications were quickly granted. Initially, the young companies were short of production capacity and sales outlets. In addition, they were not sufficiently familiar with official approval procedures for new products, and therefore sought contact with the major chemical-pharmaceutical companies. By the same token, the pharmaceutical industry was also interested in collaborating with the biotech firms, as they could provide important information on the latest developments in biomedical research. From the mid-1980s, Sandoz and Ciba-Geigy worked closely with the biotech companies, in the area of agricultural biotechnology too. In 1986, Ciba-Geigy and the Californian genetic engineering company Chiron founded a joint venture by the name of Biocine, which developed and sold new vaccines. In 1995, Sandoz acquired the US company Genetic Therapy, with which it had been pursuing joint research projects since 1991.

Ciba and Sandoz switch their focus In the late 1980s, Ciba-Geigy revised its corporate self-image and formulated a new corporate philosophy, which it named Vision 2000. This placed social and environmental goals on an equal footing with economic objectives. In strategic terms, the company – named Ciba from 1992 – remained dedicated to broad diversification, with a strong parent company running and supporting the national subsidiaries worldwide from the head office. Sandoz also sought a new orientation: in 1990, it abandoned its head-office-based structure in favor of becoming a holding company – all divisions became independent business units which acted as economically autonomous stock corporations. In making this change, Sandoz was not just implementing a new organizational model; far more, it was launching a trend which would shape the future. It gradually began to focus all its activities on the areas of pharmaceuticals, nutrition and agribusiness, with low-priority business lines being outsourced. In 1994, Sandoz acquired Gerber Products, the leading baby food manufacturer in the USA. The following year it spun off its Chemicals Division, which included dyestuffs, to form the listed company Clariant.

A coup that came out of nowhere: Sandoz and Ciba join forces The dynamic reorientation processes inspired the management of Sandoz to think in even greater dimensions: acquisition, collaboration or merger? Chairman of the Board Marc Moret (1923–2006) considered the various options – first in Europe, then in the USA – and established initial contacts. At the same time, he also looked at the possibilities for new partnerships in Switzerland and ordered internal studies on the matter. These pointed to the significant synergy potential of Sandoz and Ciba, especially in the areas of pharmaceuticals, agrochemicals and seeds. Moret decided to arrange a semi-official exploratory meeting with Ciba, which took place in his office on November 30, 1995. Moret's discussion partner was Louis von Planta, Honorary Chairman of Ciba. The talks were encouraging, and on December 4, 1995, Alex Krauer, Chairman of the Board of Ciba, indicated that he would be very interested in continuing the discussions. A plan of action was drawn up and the team members required to implement the merger project were quickly and discreetly nominated.

The top management of both companies agreed that, at a stroke, the merger offered a unique opportunity to take leading positions globally in the core sectors pharmaceuticals and agriculture. In addition, cost synergies of around 1.8 bn Swiss francs a year and considerable added value for shareholders would be achieved within three years. At its meeting of March 6, 1996, Ciba's Board of Directors declared that the "merger of the two companies" would take place "from a position of strength: both companies want this action of their own free will; neither is in crisis, as the respective balance sheets for 1995 clearly show". As the minutes state, "two equivalent partners" would engage with "a common future" in a Merger of Equals. In the meeting of the Sandoz Board of Directors on the same day, however, Robert Genillard (1929–2016) emphasized the need for the new company to take over the Sandoz company culture.

When Swiss radio station DRS (now Radio SRF) announced the merger of Ciba and Sandoz early in the morning of Thursday March 7, 1996, the presenter remarked that the report was no hoax. Managers and office and production workers had expected further acquisitions, spin-offs and relocations of entire parts of the company, but that Ciba and Sandoz – two companies with radically different corporate cultures – would agree to a merger was an unparalleled surprise. In hindsight, the large-scale merger seems to be both an expression and an accelerator of the global consolidation processes in the chemical-pharmaceutical industry.

Sandoz Nuremberg (Germany).
Packaging machinery. 1971.

Sandoz Kundl (Austria).
Work clothing. 1971.

Sandoz Dorval (Canada).
Pharmaceuticals warehouse. 1971.

Sandoz Tehran (Iran).
Packaging facilities. 1973.

Sandoz Istanbul (Turkey).
Quality control. 1973.

081
Grinding lenses at CIBA Vision in Atlanta (Georgia, USA). 1988.
As part of its diversification policy, the Ciba-Geigy Pharmaceuticals Division entered into the contact lens and lens care products market in 1981. The vision care business soon reached dimensions which justified making it independent, especially since the synergy effects with the traditional pharmaceutical business were modest. The optical lens and lens care products unit was separated from the Pharmaceuticals Division. From 1987, it became the independent group CIBA Vision.

082
Aerial photo of Basel including the St. Johann (Sandoz) and Klybeck (Ciba-Geigy) sites. 1981.

082

Ciba-Geigy Basel.
Commercial apprentice. 1977.

Ciba-Geigy Basel.
Commercial apprentice of the
internal travel agency. 1977.

Sandoz Cabo Ruivo/Lisbon
(Portugal). Packaging Ovaltine/
Ovomaltine. May 1977.

Swiss Nigerian Chemical Company
in Lagos (Nigeria).
Pharmaceuticals production.
1988.

Sandoz Witterswil (Switzerland).
Agrobiological research station.
1984.

083
Production at Wasa in Filipstad (Sweden).
Probably 1994.
In 1982, Sandoz acquired the Swedish group
Wasa, the world's largest manufacturer
of crispbread. This significantly strengthened
the position of the nutrition department
within the corporation.

084
Ferrari with red Ciba-Geigy pigment. 1990.
In 1986, the Plastics and Additives Division of
the Ciba-Geigy group launched a new red
pigment for automotive paints. The car paint
industry reacted quickly and positively.

083

084

Ciba-Geigy Santiago de Chile.
Packaging. 1987.

Ciba-Geigy Kemps Creek/Sydney.
Agrochemical research laboratory.
1987.

Ciba-Geigy Manila (Philippines).
Reception. 1987.

Ciba-Geigy Athens (Greece).
Pharmaceutical production. 1988.

Ciba-Geigy Arnhem (Netherlands).
Dyestuff laboratory. 1988.

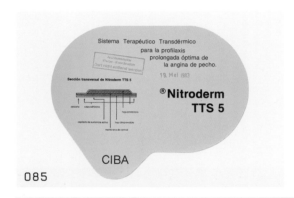

085

085
Chilean *Nitroderm TTS* brochure. 1983.
In 1978, Ciba-Geigy began collaborating with
US company ALZA Corporation. Together,
they developed three transdermal therapeutic system (TTS) products: *Scopoderm TTS*
for nausea and vomiting due to travel sickness, *Nitroderm TTS* for long-term treatment
of angina pectoris and *Estraderm TTS* for
alleviating postmenopausal complaints.

086
Interferon test at Ciba-Geigy. 1985.

087
**Biotechnology research workers at Ciba-
Geigy in Basel with a structural model of the
molecule interleukin-1 beta. 1990.**

086

087

143

CIBA Vision Atlanta (Georgia, USA).
Casting lenses. 1988.

Ciba-Geigy Isando/Johannesburg
(South Africa). Packaging. 1988.

Ciba-Geigy Origgio (Italy).
Gate staff. 1988.

Ciba-Geigy Rueil-Malmaison
(France). Canteen. 1989.

Ciba-Geigy Tongi (Bangladesh).
Staff training. 1990.

088
**Sandoz production site in Ringaskiddy,
near Cork (Ireland) during construction. 1992.**
In 1995, Sandoz opened what was at the
time the world's most modern and environ-
mentally friendly production site for active
pharmaceutical substances.

089
Marc Moret (1923–2006). 1986.
Marc Moret was born in Ménières (Switzerland) and studied economics in Fribourg
(Switzerland) and Paris, gaining a doctorate
in 1948. His career took him via various
medium- and large-sized companies
(including Nestlé) to Sandoz in 1968, where
he initially headed up sales and marketing in
agrochemicals, and later the agrochemicals
and the agrochemicals/nutrition departments. In 1976, he became head of corporate
finance. In 1977, he was elected to the
Sandoz Board of Directors and appointed
Executive Member of the Board, and in 1980
he became Vice Chairman. Moret took over
operational management of the Sandoz Group
in May 1981 as Chairman of the Executive
Committee. In 1985, he was elected Chairman
of the Board of Directors. Although Moret
formally gave up managing the company
in 1993, he remained its key figure thanks
to his role as Chairman of the Board.
Moret made economic history in 1996 when
he engineered the merger of Sandoz and
Ciba to form Novartis. After he retired from
an active role, he was named Honorary
Chairman of Novartis.

089

Ciba-Geigy Takarazuka (Japan).
Protein analysis. 1991.

Ciba-Geigy Buenos Aires
(Argentina). Pharmaceutical
quality control. 1990.

Ciba-Geigy Greensboro
(North Carolina, USA).
Dyestuff research laboratory.
1990.

Sandoz East Hanover
(New Jersey, USA). IT system.
1992.

Ciba-Geigy Grenzach (Germany).
Operations staff from building
9076. 1993.

090

Alex Krauer. 1987.
Alex Krauer was born in Basel in 1931.
After gaining his university entrance qualification at school, he studied economics
at the Universities of Basel and Paris and at
the London School of Economics. In 1955,
he was awarded a doctorate by the University
of Basel. He joined the finance department
of CIBA in 1956, where he initially worked
as head of accounting and later as head of
finance and administration in the Italian
group company of CIBA/Ciba-Geigy. When he
returned to Switzerland in 1972, he took
over management of the central control and
management services function in Basel.
He became a member of the Executive
Committee in 1976. In 1982, he was appointed
Deputy Chairman of this committee, and
from 1987 to 1995 he was Chairman and CEO
of Ciba-Geigy. Following the merger of
Ciba and Sandoz to form Novartis he worked
as Chairman of the Board until 1999.
Since then he has been Honorary Chairman
of Novartis.

091 | 092
**Changing the logo at the Novartis St. Johann
site in Basel. February 3, 1997.**

090

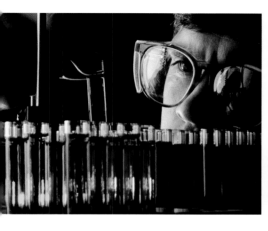

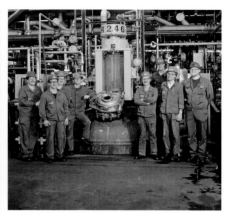

091

092

SANDIMMUNE

A fungus to inhibit the immune system

In the 1960s, it was customary for scientists to return from their travels with soil samples. From these, the laboratories in natural substances departments would then routinely isolate fungi and bacteria. Microorganisms form an abundance of natural substances still studied today by pharmaceutical researchers in order to discover therapeutically interesting active substances. This was how, in the summer of 1969, Sandoz discovered a fungus (*Tolypocladium inflatum*) in "holiday soil" from the Hardangervidda, a Norwegian plateau. While it did not show any antibacterial effects in the various tests, it did inhibit the growth of other fungi. The active substance was analyzed and identified as a new type of cyclic peptide (a circular protein from two or more amino acids). It subsequently turned out that the compound – later named cyclosporine – demonstrates highly specific suppression of cells that play a key role in the immune system.

Immunosuppression is desirable in the case of certain diseases in which the immune system attacks the body's own tissue (autoimmune diseases) and for organ transplants. After a transplant, the immune system normally attempts to reject the new organ because it recognizes it as foreign tissue. Cyclosporine has the important property of inhibiting immune cells which are key to rejecting foreign tissue, while still allowing the immune system to defend against infection. This sets the new immunosuppressant apart from classic cytostatic substances, such as azathioprine, which non-specifically inhibit all cells from dividing.

At Sandoz, the decision to begin developing cyclosporine opened up a second key area of natural substance research after ergot alkaloids – the search for new immunosuppressants. This step was a decisive contribution to the establishment of a new research field in transplantation medicine. Preclinical development revealed that cyclosporine does not reach the blood when administered in capsules. This setback prompted scientists to investigate on themselves which dosage form would allow the substance to be best absorbed by the body. Ultimately, they discovered that a mixture containing olive oil is the most suitable. After many preclinical and clinical studies, transplants in animals and trial treatments in patients, the first pharmacological publication on cyclosporine appeared in 1976. The compound was first launched on the market in 1982 under the trade name *Sandimmune*, followed by *Neoral*, an improved formulation in a microemulsion, in 1994. These medicines enabled a breakthrough in transplantation medicine and, over three decades, have saved, extended or improved thousands of people's lives. In addition to kidney, heart, liver, lung, pancreas, bone marrow and tissue transplants, cyclosporine also proved to be extremely effective as a treatment for autoimmune diseases such as psoriasis and rheumatoid arthritis.

1
Vials containing *Sandimmune* oral solution. Probably 1992–1993.

2
Infusion ampoules with sterile *Sandimmune* solution. Probably 1992–1993.

3
Packaging of *Sandimmune* and *Neoral*. 1980s and 1990s.

1

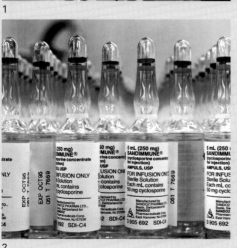

2

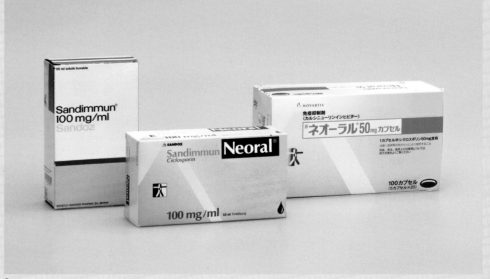

3

TEGRETOL AND TRILEPTAL

Safety for epileptics

Few illnesses have been met with more revulsion, fear and superstition than epilepsy (once known as falling sickness). Whereas the disease was (and sometimes still is) viewed in some cultures as a punishment by dark forces, epilepsy sufferers are revered in other cultures as "chosen ones". Even in industrialized societies, attitudes toward epilepsy are still far from being free of prejudice and misconception. In addition to the illness itself, sufferers often have to contend with discrimination, ostracism and problems in the workplace. But epilepsy patients, who make up around 1 per cent of the world population, are "ordinary" people who occasionally suffer from certain "extraordinary" symptoms: they suffer epileptic seizures caused by a temporary increase in the activity of certain groups of brain cells. Epilepsy is not a mental illness, but a neurological disorder probably attributable to hereditary brain damage or brain injury. The symptoms and severity of epilepsy can vary considerably: generalized seizures affect the entire cerebral cortex and are often associated with loss of consciousness, whereas focal seizures arise in restricted regions of the brain.

Modern epilepsy treatment began in 1857 when Sir Charles Locock demonstrated the anti-epileptic effect of potassium bromide. The bromide substance class alleviates epileptic seizures by sedating the functions of the central nervous system. Chemists continued their research on this basis until phenobarbital became available, a sedative and hypnotic whose anti-epileptic effect was known from 1912. The broadly effective phenobarbital soon became so firmly established in clinical practice that, as late as 1987, one-third of all epileptics were still being treated with medication containing this active substance. The subsequent generation of antiepileptics was the result of a better understanding of the pathology of epilepsy. Animal models were helpful here: it was recognized that animals react to certain electrical and chemical stimuli with epileptic seizures. Consequently, research on animals has enabled a targeted search for new epilepsy treatments and their development to clinical maturity.

An excellent example of the breakthrough that these models achieved is the development of carbamazepine. In 1957, Geigy managed to synthesize this compound from a series of ureas. Carbamazepine was patented in Switzerland in the same year and proved to be a highly effective and very well tolerated anticonvulsant. Its broad clinical spectrum was recognized at the same time: carbamazepine is effective not only for generalized and simple focal seizures, but also for the previously hard-to-treat temporal lobe epilepsy and a host of other neurological disorders. This innovative medicine was first launched on the Swiss and UK markets in 1963, under the name *Tegretol*, and was eventually registered in around 150 countries. By the turn of the millennium it had become established as a mainstay epilepsy treatment, being used in some 15 per cent of all epilepsy cases. In the meantime, *Tegretol* has undergone successful further developments and been launched as a new anti-epileptic under the trade name *Trileptal*. This is just as effective as *Tegretol*, but better tolerated and easier to dose.

1
Advertisement for *Tegretol* (carbamazepine B.P.) for childhood epilepsy. 1970s.

A major advantage of *Trileptal* is that it has fewer interactions with other drugs. However, its development was more difficult than that of *Tegretol*.

Oxcarbazepine – the active substance in *Trileptal* – had already been synthesized in 1966, but its effect potential remained undiscovered until the mid-1970s. When Ciba-Geigy scientists renewed the search for a new anti-epileptic, one of the substances they studied was oxcarbazepine, and they recognized its advantages from animal experiments. Although initial clinical studies were disappointing, the researchers did not give up. They ultimately discovered that a higher dosage was required than with *Tegretol* in order to achieve comparable results. Positive outcomes enabled the drug to be launched on the market – in 1990 in Denmark, in 1999 throughout the EU and in 2000 in the USA.

It is in large measure thanks to pioneering medicines such as *Tegretol* and *Trileptal* that, today, 60–80 per cent of all children and adults newly diagnosed with epilepsy can be successfully treated with medication that brings seizures completely under control.

Tegretol®
carbamazepine BP

in childhood epilepsy

1

8   NOVARTIS

FROM LIFE SCIENCES TO FOCUS ON INNOVATIVE MEDICINE 1996–2021

Since the second half of the 1990s, the number of people in the world has increased from 5.8 billion to nearly 8 billion. Not only increased life expectancy for individuals, but also the constant increase in the world population have strongly fueled demand for healthcare services and products. Further reasons for this development are advances in diagnostics and research into the causes of illnesses, new possibilities of treatment for previously incurable diseases or ones which were hard to cure, and the medical backlog in threshold and developing countries.

A single company: focus on integration When Novartis was formed on December 20, 1996, the largest company merger in the history of the industry at that time was entered in the Basel Commercial Register. The name is inspired by the Latin *novae artes*, meaning "new arts, new skills". The merger was one of equals and took place by means of a stock swap, i.e. with no payment of takeover premiums. For this reason, the Board of Directors (16 members) and the Executive Committee (8 members) comprised equal numbers of leading figures from Ciba and Sandoz. Alex Krauer (Ciba) became Chairman of the Board of Directors, and Daniel Vasella (Sandoz) CEO and Executive Member of the Board of Directors. The leaders involved attached great importance to amalgamating Sandoz and Ciba to form Novartis as rapidly as possible. Planning of the merger process lasted until April 1996. Subsequently, an integration office took on the role of coordinating and guiding the 200 special taskforces and 600 project teams through the integration process. Before officially completing the merger, 3,500 management positions had to be assigned, the global organizational structures and staffing levels defined, business processes evaluated and locations selected. As early as 1998, the integration process was largely completed. In April 1999, Krauer retired and Vasella took over the role of Novartis Chairman, whilst also remaining CEO until 2010.

Three business areas: focus on life sciences When Ciba and Sandoz merged, both groups were completely restructured. From then on, Novartis devoted itself to three business areas within life sciences: healthcare, agribusiness and nutrition. This strategic focus required the spin-off of the industrial divisions. In 1996, the precision balances manufacturer Mettler Toledo and the construction chemicals firm MBT were divested. Ciba's other industrial divisions were merged in 1997 to form the new company Ciba Specialty Chemicals, which was listed on the stock exchange.

The key to success: innovation as strategy Right from the start, Novartis declared its intention to become a market leader in all three of its business areas. The merger gave it a more broad-based market presence with a network of large sales organizations spanning the globe. Research and development were also called upon to sustain growth in all divisions through innovative products. To strengthen its internal research capabilities, alliances were forged and cooperation agreements sought with research institutes and biotech companies. In La Jolla (California, USA), the group founded the Genomics Institute of the Novartis Research Foundation.

A brilliant start: synergies and restructuring In its first year, Novartis achieved superb results, with the group's net profit rising by 43 per cent to 5.2 billion Swiss francs. This brilliant start was due in no small way to the synergy effects of the merger, with cost savings of 2 billion Swiss francs being made between 1996 and 1998. In 1998, the group commenced wide-ranging restructuring measures: the self-medication unit of the Pharmaceuticals Division was merged with the Nutrition Division to form the new Consumer Health Division. This grouped together the three businesses of over-the-counter, health and functional nutrition (including Gerber with its infant nutrition segment) and medical nutrition. In parallel, Novartis began to sell off certain parts of the company, including health food store brand Eden and the crispbread manufacturer Wasa.

Towards the end of the millennium, the agricultural business lost a significant amount of ground due to adverse market trends: in 1999, it recorded a 7 per cent decline in sales. But the Pharmaceuticals Division also posted less dynamic growth. Key products such as *Voltaren* and *Sandimmune* lost traction due to expiring patents. With growth of just 4 per cent, sales momentum within the Pharmaceuticals Division in 1999 was significantly below the overall market average. It was now time to replace the "blockbusters" which were no longer under patent protection with new, innovative medications. This required two areas of focus: bundling strengths in the pharmaceutical sector and invigorating research and development.

Spin-off of agribusiness: the founding of Syngenta In 1999, the Board of Directors decided to spin off the crop protection and seeds businesses. They were merged with the agribusiness of the Anglo-Swedish group Astra-Zeneca in 2000, thus creating the first company ever to focus entirely on agriculture: Syngenta, headquartered in Basel. Novartis retained the animal health unit and made it part of the Consumer Health Division. The spin-off of its agricultural business saw the life sciences concept abandoned in favor of concentrating on the healthcare sector. The marginal synergies between the agricultural and health businesses had not compensated for the differences between them.

Turnaround at the turn of the millennium – innovation as the elixir of life In 2001, Novartis achieved double-digit sales growth, and also managed to increase operating income within the Pharmaceuticals Division by a further 8 per cent, despite making additional investments in new launches and key products. This development was mainly thanks to the pharmaceutical business in the USA, where sales growth of 24 per cent was achieved. This was due not only to putting a great deal of effort into the expansion of sales and marketing, but also to significantly increasing the number of visits to doctors. Furthermore, the consistent strategy of innovation bore fruit: 2001 was the second consecutive year in which the US authorities granted more marketing authorizations to Novartis for new active substances than to any of its competitors. The products registered in record time included *Gleevec/Glivec*, the revolutionary treatment for chronic myeloid leukemia. At the same time, *Diovan*, a very effective and well-tolerated antihypertensive, grew to become a key revenue driver due to its pharmacological profile. In 2002, through systematic investments, the company founded the Novartis Institutes for BioMedical Research (NIBR) in Cambridge (Massachusetts, USA). At the end of 2009, the group announced its intention to build a new research campus in Shanghai.

Novartis invests in Basel-based competitor Roche In 2001, Novartis took over around 20 per cent of the bearer shares of F. Hoffmann-La Roche AG from BZ Group Holding AG, Zurich. Up to 2003, Novartis increased its holding to 33 per cent. The purchase of the holding and its subsequent increase fueled wild speculation in Basel that another megamerger – namely between Novartis and Roche – was on the cards. These prophecies have not been fulfilled so far. Novartis, however, has retained the substantial holding as a secure financial investment.

Focused diversification: Sandoz, Vaccines & Diagnostics and Alcon After the turn of the millennium, Novartis pursued a strategy of focused diversification, concentrating consistently on healthcare. Consequently, it sold the Health & Functional Food unit in 2002, and in so doing said goodbye to the legendary Ovaltine/Ovomaltine brand. At the same time, Novartis acquired the Slovenian generics group Lek. In addition, it started to consolidate all its business with off-patent medicines under the Sandoz name. In 2005, Novartis bought and integrated the German generics provider Hexal together with the US company Eon Labs, Inc. One year later, Novartis acquired the remaining shares in vaccines producer Chiron, and created the new Vaccines & Diagnostics Division. In 2007, Novartis sold its medical nutrition and Gerber business units to Swiss food corporation Nestlé. In 2011, Novartis completed its focus on wide-ranging healthcare activities: it gained 100 per cent ownership of Alcon, in which it had held a majority since 2010. This allowed the amalgamation of the Alcon business with the activities of CIBA Vision and the Novartis ophthalmics portfolio to form a new division in the group.

Strengthening of Corporate Governance – Novartis as transparent and trustworthy partner The departure of Daniel Vasella as Chairman in 2013 and the arrival of Joerg Reinhardt signalled a turning point at Novartis. The Chairman's Committee, which under Vasella had prepared the decisions of the Board of Directors, was dissolved. At the same time, the Board of Directors gave the Executive Committee greater powers in order to accelerate decision-making processes. The supreme executive body also created a new committee, the Research and Development Committee (now Science and Technology Committee), which monitors the strategies and organization of research and development efforts. In addition, it extended the mandate of the Corporate Governance and Nomination Committee to the area of Corporate Responsibility. In 2014, Novartis introduced a new internal ethics organization located with the Executive Committee and equipped with many resources. These steps aimed to create greater transparency and trust, thereby enhancing the image of the company in society. In February 2018, Vasant Narasimhan took over as Head of the Executive Committee. The new CEO came with the aspiration of replacing the former hierarchical structures and processes and establishing a new company culture.

Company reorganization – on two instead of six legs In 2014, Novartis introduced the largest reorganization since the merger of Ciba and Sandoz. In a multilevel process, the group moved away from the strategy of focused diversification. The low-profit animal health and the unprofitable vaccine businesses were sold, and the over-the-counter unit became part of a joint venture with GlaxoSmithKline (GSK). At the same time, Novartis took over the GSK oncology business and thus expanded its position in cancer treatment. As a result, Novartis concentrated on just three business areas: Innovative Medicines (the former Pharmaceuticals Division), eye care (Alcon) and generics (Sandoz). The reorganization soon entered the next phase. In 2018, Novartis gave up its involvement in the joint venture with GSK. After the ophthalmological medications were moved from Alcon and integrated into the pharmaceuticals sector of the group in 2016, Novartis withdrew from the contact lens and surgical instruments business in 2019. The eyecare division was spun off and listed on the stock exchange as an independent company. Thus a further step in the formation of a focused drug company was completed – to be active only in areas where Novartis belongs to the world's best. This new direction should be seen against the background that a number of top-selling medicines had come off patent (e.g. *Diovan*) or were soon to (e.g. *Gleevec/Glivec*). The basic reorganization of the group had the aim of strengthening Novartis' sales and profit growth together with its innovative capabilities. On the other hand, the group saw itself compelled to monitor costs more closely. So in 2014, the company began the formation of a central services organization: business support functions like IT, real estate and buildings management, procurement, personnel services, the operative financial reporting and accounting were consolidated in the new unit Novartis Business Services (called Customer and Technology Solutions from 2021). A large part of the activities was newly allotted to global service centers located in inexpensive countries like the Czech Republic or India.

Investments in groundbreaking technologies Revolutionary developments in research and digitalization will change medicine in the 21st century faster than ever before – and health services too. Novartis therefore invested large sums in cutting-edge technologies, above all in cell, gene and radioligand therapies. To this end, Novartis acquired the gene therapy specialist AveXis together with the radiopharmaceutical companies Advanced Accelerator Applications and Endocyte in 2018. Furthermore, Novartis deepened its activities in the data and digital areas by initiating various cooperations with leading technology partners. For instance, it reached an agreement for cooperation with the software company Microsoft in the field of artificial intelligence. The use of cutting-edge technologies was all the more important because the costs for the development of a new active substance had nearly doubled since 2010. The availability and the enhanced possibilities of leveraging Big Data (artificial intelligence) will make the development of medicines faster and less expensive.

Novartis Caracas (Venezuela).
Community Partnership Day.
April 1998.

Novartis Ho Chi Minh City
(Vietnam). Community Partnership
Day. 2016.

093
Daniel Vasella. May 2002.
Daniel Vasella was born in 1953 in Fribourg
(Switzerland). He graduated in medicine from
the University of Bern (Switzerland) in 1979,
completing his doctoral thesis in clinical
pharmacology in 1980. During the 1980s
he worked as a physician in various hospitals,
ultimately as senior physician for internal
medicine at the Inselspital Bern. He changed
career in 1988, moving into industry, and
worked for four years in the USA in the
marketing department at Sandoz Pharmaceuticals. In 1992, he returned to Switzerland
as assistant to the Chief Operating Officer
(COO) of the Pharmaceuticals Division, later
becoming head of corporate product management. In 1994, Sandoz appointed him COO
of the Pharmaceuticals Division and he was
assigned responsibility for global development in this sector. He took over as head of
the Pharmaceuticals Division in 1995,
becoming a member of the Executive Committee. The merger of Sandoz and Ciba made
Vasella Executive Member of the Board of
Directors and CEO of Novartis. From 1999,
he also had the role of Chairman of the Board
of Directors. Vasella passed on the position
of CEO to Joseph Jimenez in 2010. At the
General Meeting held on February 22, 2013,
Vasella did not stand for re-election. On
August 1, 2013, Joerg Reinhardt succeeded
him on the Board and as Chairman of the
Board.

094
**Novartis Basel. Laboratory at Fabrikstrasse
16. February 2008.**

093

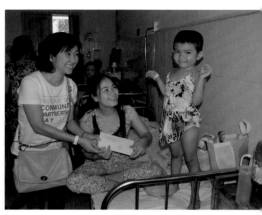

Novartis Basel. Associates from
Visitor Services. 2001.

Lek Mengeš (Slovenia).
A researcher changes clothing
to work in the development
laboratory. 2017.

095
**Novartis Wehr (Germany). Laboratory.
December 2001.**

096
**Vasant Narasimhan (CEO since 2018) and
Joerg Reinhardt. May 26, 2015.**
Joerg Reinhardt was born in 1956 in Homburg
(Germany). He studied pharmacy at Saarland
University and obtained his doctorate in
1981. Reinhardt began his professional
career in 1982 at Sandoz AG, where he was
engaged in various positions of increasing
responsibility in Research and Development,
finishing up as global Head of Development.
After the founding of Novartis, Reinhardt was
at first responsible for Preclinical Development. In 1999, he became Head of Development in the Pharmaceuticals Division. In this
role, he was responsible for clinical, pharmaceutical, chemical and biotechnological
product development, testing of drug safety,
and regulatory affairs. From 2006 to 2008,
Reinhardt headed the Vaccines & Diagnostics Division. In 2008, he became Chief Operating Officer of the Novartis Group. In 2010,
Reinhardt moved to Bayer HealthCare AG
in Leverkusen (Germany), where he was
Chairman of the Board of Management and
the Executive Committee until 2013. From
2012 to 2013 he sat on the Board of Directors
of Lonza Group AG, Basel, and since 2017
on the Board of Swiss Re AG, Zurich.
On August 1, 2013 Reinhardt took over as
Chairman of the Board of Novartis AG.
Joerg Reinhardt is the architect of the reorganization that heralded Novartis' departure
from Daniel Vasella's broadly diversified
growth strategy.

097
**Novartis lists its shares on the New York
Stock Exchange. May 11, 2000.**

095

096

097

Novartis Basel. Company
archive. 2010.

Novartis Horsham (UK).
Laboratory. November 2001.

Sandoz Schaftenau (Austria).
Biosimilars production. 2016.

098
Packaging of *Fortekor*. Around 2001.
What is effective in humans often works in
animals too. There are synergies in numerous
indications. The active substance in *Fortekor,*
benazepril hydrochloride, is also contained
in the medicine *Cibacen* (ACE inhibitor)
for lowering blood pressure in humans and is
prescribed for dogs with heart failure.
Fortekor is approved for cats with kidney
problems (chronic renal insufficiency) as well.

099
Novartis Saint-Aubin (Switzerland). 2009.
The Centre de Recherche Santé Animale
in Saint-Aubin was one of the most important
research facilities of Novartis Animal
Health worldwide. Screening is crucial to
successful research. This is a sifting
and selection process in which the effect of
active substances is tested in the laboratory.

100
Klybeck Site. October 2017.
Since the turn of the millennium, a reshaping
and reconstruction of larger rail and industrial sites has been taking place in the City of
Basel, where land resources are scarce.
That includes the sites of the former Ciba-
Geigy in Klybeck and Rosental. For some
time, the Klybeck site had hardly been needed for industrial production, and some of the
laboratory and office buildings were standing
empty too. In 2016, Novartis and BASF,
the owners of the land, therefore reached a
planning agreement with the Canton of
Basel-City on a new use for the site. On a
total area of 280,000 square meters, a new
urban district is to emerge, with different
uses for residence, work, leisure and culture.
In 2019, Novartis sold its part of the site
(160,000 square meters) to Central Real
Estate AG Basel, which is backed by Swiss
investors (insurance companies and pension
funds). In the same year, the insurance
company Swiss Life acquired BASF's part
of the site. Both partners took over the con-
tractual obligations of the planning agreement of 2016.

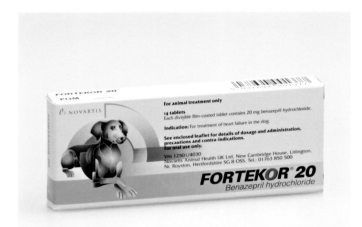

098

099

Friedrich Miescher Institute for
Biomedical Research Basel. 2010.

The Novartis Institute for Tropical
Diseases in Singapore. June 2004.

101
Media conference for the founding of the IOB (Institute of Molecular and Clinical Ophthalmology Basel). December 15, 2017.
In December 2017, the University of Basel founded a joint research facility with the University Hospital of Basel and Novartis. The IOB's aims are to improve the understanding of eye diseases and develop therapeutic approaches, so research and clinical application are closely linked. Novartis is bearing half the costs in the first ten years, the other founding partners and the Canton of Basel-City the rest.

102
Novartis Campus in Shanghai (China). 2016.

103
Novartis Cambridge (Massachusetts, USA). 2009.
Novartis Institutes for BioMedical Research (NIBR) in Cambridge received an Energy Excellence Award in 2007 for its ingenious energy conservation programme. The award-winning concept is all-embracing. It ranges from lighting and air-conditioning parameters through modernized building control systems to a code of conduct for associates.

103

Novartis Behring Marburg
(Germany). Vaccine production
associate. 2010.

Novartis Nyon (Canton Vaud,
Switzerland). OTC Division
Production. 2013.

Novartis Pharmanalytica Locarno
(Switzerland). Analytical laboratory. 2009.

Novartis Basel. Vocational trainer
with apprentice (biology laboratory technician, 3rd year of
apprenticeship). 2009.

Novartis associates in Turkey on
a Coartem training course. 2015.

104
Russian packaging of Myfortic. After 2002.

105
Gilenya **capsules. 2011.**
Gilenya, the first medicine in a new therapeutic class of so-called S1P receptor
modulators, has the potential to revolu-
tionize the treatment of multiple sclerosis
(MS). Novartis acquired FTY720 in 1997
from a Japanese company to test the substance in transplantation medicine.

106
**Associates of the Ghana Telemedicine
Program (Ghana). 2018.**
From the very beginning, Novartis recognized
social responsibility as an integral compo-
nent of its corporate strategy. In this spirit,
it continues the Foundation for Sustainable
Development (now called the Novartis
Foundation), which Ciba-Geigy began in 1979.
As part of various programs, the Foundation
does a great deal worldwide to ease access
to local healthcare provision for people
on low incomes. The Ghana Telemedicine
Program, for example, uses information
and communication technology to connect
local health service personnel with medical
specialists via 24-hour teleconsultation
centers: doctors, nurses and midwives in
teleconsultation centers give coaching
to local, often rural health service providers.
This not only improves the quality of patient
care, but also avoids unnecessary hospital-
izations. With the COVID-19-pandemic,
the demand for telemedicine has risen dra-
matically and its integration in health services is rapidly accelerating.

104

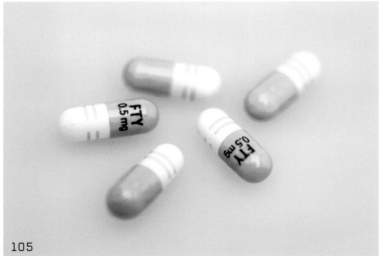
105

106

NOVARTIS CAMPUS

Melting pot for innovations
in medicine

The merger of Ciba and Sandoz meant Novartis had three extensive locations in Basel: Rosental, Klybeck and St. Johann. After the spin-off of the Agricultural Division in 2000, the Rosental site became the new headquarters of Syngenta. For its part, Novartis established the St. Johann site as a location for Research and Development, Marketing and the Executive Committee. This avoided unnecessary travel and duplication, and optimized collaboration.

Located in northern Basel next to the French border, the St. Johann site had developed remarkably quickly from 1886 onwards, but in a somewhat piecemeal fashion. At the end of the 20th century, it was a rather random collection of buildings with various purposes, styles and in different states of repair. Major investment was required for the site to meet modern environmental and working standards.

The outsourcing of most production activity away from the city and the constant expansion of Research and Development, Marketing and Administration brought about a profound change in the needs of employees. Daniel Vasella, Chairman and CEO of Novartis at that time, declared that his goal was to transform the industrial site – which had previously been centered around machines – into a campus that would be attractive for people. Innovation and performance were to be boosted by communication, collaboration and both planned and spontaneous meetings. The new work environment needed to be attractive to job applicants and employees and make them feel at ease. To achieve this vision, in 2001 the Board of Directors asked the architect and urbanist Vittorio Magnago Lampugnani to draw up a master plan for the Campus. To begin the implementation, Novartis enlisted the services of landscape architect Peter Walker, art curator Harald Szeemann, lighting designer Andreas Schulz, graphic designer Alan Fletcher and industrial psychologist Fritz Steele.

Based on the goals set, this master plan focused on open spaces "that create a feeling of well-being and stimulate communication", around which are grouped "buildings whose use is flexible and not predefined". To avoid uniformity of design, every new building was designed and then also built by a different architect. The selected structures were to be elegant and unobtrusive in style and through their diversity reflect the cultures of the chosen architects. Based on these positive experiences, Novartis implemented similar campus projects in Shanghai (China) and Cambridge (USA).

Today, around 7,500 people work at the Campus in Basel, where 17 renowned architects or teams of architects constructed buildings:
- Roger Diener, Basel; Gerold Wiederin, Vienna; Helmut Federle, Vienna: Forum 3 (2005)
- Kazuyo Sejima & Ryue Nishizawa (SANAA), Tokyo: Fabrikstrasse 4 (2006)
- Peter Märkli, Zurich: Visitor Center Fabrikstrasse 6 (2006)
- Marco Serra, Basel: Entrance pavilion Fabrikstrasse 2 and underground car park (2007); underground parking for 800 bicycles (2018)
- Adolf Krischanitz, Vienna; Berlin; Zurich: Fabrikstrasse 16 (2008)

1
First sketch of the master plan.
February 2001.

2
Partial view of Fabrikstrasse. 2009.

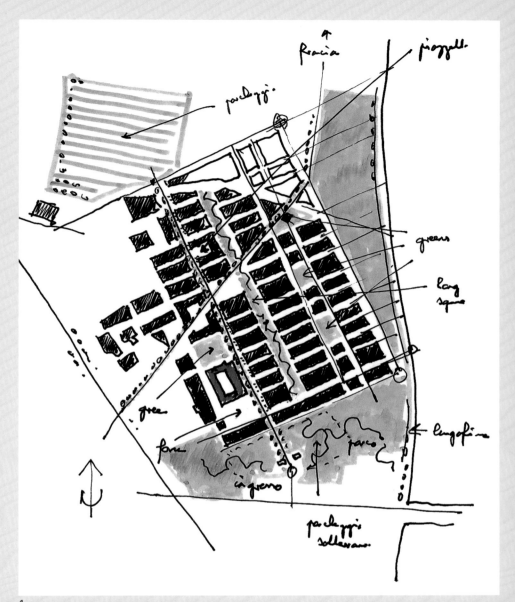

1

2

171

— Vittorio Magnago Lampugnani, Milan: Fabrikstrasse 12 (2008)
— José Rafael Moneo Vallés, Madrid: Fabrikstrasse 14 (2009)
— Frank O. Gehry, Los Angeles: Fabrikstrasse 15 (2009)
— Fumihiko Maki, Tokyo: Square 3 (2009)
— Tadao Ando, Osaka: Fabrikstrasse 28 (2010)
— David Chipperfield, London: Fabrikstrasse 22 (2010)
— Yoshio Taniguchi, Tokyo: Fabrikstrasse 10 (2010)
— Eduardo Souto de Moura, Porto: Physic Garden 3 (2011)
— Álvaro Siza, Porto: Virchow 6 (2011)
— Juan Navarro Baldeweg, Madrid: Fabrikstrasse 18 (2014)
— Rahul Mehrotra, Mumbai/Boston: Virchow 16 (2015)
— Herzog & de Meuron, Basel: Asklepios 8 (2015)

At the northern end of Fabrikstrasse, the large multipart sculpture by Richard Serra marks the vanishing point from the main entrance in the south and the northern access point to the 20-hectare site. Many works by internationally eminent artists enhance the buildings, squares and parks. The roads that cross the length and breadth of the Campus honor significant figures from medical history, bearing the names of individuals whose achievements have played an important role in the fields of activity in which Novartis operates.

Shaped by Peter Walker and others, Fabrikstrasse, 600 meters long, was refurbished into a tree-lined avenue which has become the backbone of this new urban structure. Lampugnani's vision was to create a modern version of the Rue de Rivoli in Paris, "lined on one side by a row of trees, and on the other by elegant arcades under which cafés, restaurants and shops will open".

Since 2012, the "Physic Garden" reminds us of the origins of the pharmaceutical industry: designed by landscape architect Thorbjörn Andersson, this green area re-interprets the medieval cloister garden. It comprises a collection of around 80 different medicinal plants which the Natural Substance Department team put together from many different parts of the world; an oasis of colors and aromas was created, to linger and relax in the middle of a building complex.

At the entrance to the Campus is a park designed by Günther Vogt that links the green area of the existing Voltamatte city park with the relaxation zone along the banks of the river Rhine. As a gift to the public on the occasion of the company's 25th anniversary, a new building by the architect Michele de Lucchi will open at the end of 2021 next to the head of the Dreirosenbrücke ("Three Roses Bridge"). The building, called the "Novartis Pavillon", will be a meeting and exchange location for the general population. On the upper floor, the public and school classes can enjoy interactive presentations that portray Novartis' current therapeutic areas and research and development techniques, the history of the chemical and pharmaceutical industry in Basel, and the future perspectives for cutting-edge medicine. Just beside it beckons a wave-like terraced "Rhine Promenade", with a public restaurant and cycle- and footpaths stretching two kilometers to the Three Countries Bridge in France.

Novartis is constantly monitoring how the vision for the Campus in Basel should be developed further. Presently, the aim is to create an open environment for innovation, where a global company and important science and technology partners can work together. At the end of 2019, Chairman of the Board of Directors Joerg Reinhardt announced that the "forbidden city" – as the Campus had been nicknamed – would open up step by step. To ease the interaction with players in the areas of digital health, biotechnology or industrial transformation as well as society and the local community, companies and institutions from related sectors – including the Friedrich Miescher Institute – should locate themselves on the Novartis Campus. In this way, shared workplaces can generate lively networks between companies and start-ups and at the same time integrate areas of exchange. This will help bring innovative ideas in healthcare to fruition.

3

4

5

DIOVAN AND ENTRESTO

Cascade inhibitors
as leaps in innovation

According to the World Health Organization (WHO), cardiovascular diseases are the number one cause of death worldwide. These "diseases of civilization" have gradually replaced illnesses like typhoid, smallpox, cholera, tuberculosis or the now relatively easily treatable diseases like intestinal infections or pneumonia as the most common causes of death. Their many different manifestations call for innovative therapies even today.

Starting out from the pathological and physiological investigations of the cardiovascular system by19th century researchers, the biochemical background began to be clarified in the research laboratories of tertiary institutions and the pharmaceutical industry from the middle of the 20th century. The main focus at that time was on peptides. These are relatively short sequences of amino acids, small proteins so to speak. As hormones they can, for instance, take over the regulation of biochemical-physiological functions or as enzymes initiate and accelerate metabolic processes.

One of these peptides is angiotensin II. In the 1950s, it was discovered that it constricts the blood vessels and thus plays a decisive part in regulating blood pressure. Step by step, the mechanism was clarified. Angiotensinogen, a hormone precursor originating in the liver, is first split by renin, an enzyme from the kidneys, to form the hormone precursor angiotensin I. What is known as the ACE (angiotensin converting enzyme) then transforms that into angiotensin II. If this fastens on to the angiotensin receptors, it leads among other things to regulation of the steroid hormone aldosterone and thereby the sodium and water balance.

The elucidation of this mechanism, known as the RAAS (renin-angiotensin-aldosterone system), allowed the development of the first drugs to treat high blood pressure. In the 1970s, for instance, ACE inhibitors were developed to block ACE activity.

The angiotensin receptors at the end of the chain offered a further target. Since 1996, Ciba-Geigy had successfully marketed the molecule valsartan, an angiotensin receptor blocker (ARB), under the name of *Diovan*. It prevailed against similar competitor products due to its longer efficacy and better tolerance. *Diovan* thus increased its sales every year. When its patent expired in 2012, it was generating between five and six billion US dollars a year.

Diovan turned out to reduce cardiovascular mortality too, if administered after a heart attack. This conclusion was reached in 2003 by the largest long-term controlled study (VALIANT) ever conducted in individuals who had survived a heart attack. As a result, in 2002, the US Food and Drug Administration (FDA) extended *Diovan's* indications to include heart failure, and the European Medicines Agency followed suit three years later.

Heart failure occurs when the heart is no longer able to pump sufficient blood through the body. Provision for the inner organs is therefore no longer guaranteed and the muscles are starved of oxygen, leading to water retention, breathlessness, rapid fatigue or even sudden cardiac arrest.

1
Diovan production in Wehr (Germany).
December 2001.

As early as the 1970s, a further peptide class was investigated which likewise regulates the water and electrolyte balance and thereby blood pressure: these are known as natriuretic peptides. Among other things, they excrete sodium via the kidneys when the heart is under pressure from too high a volume of blood. This reduces the blood volume and eases pressure on the heart. Some enzymes, for example neprilysin, limit this counter-regulation by rapidly breaking down the natriuretic peptides in the blood. Successfully inhibiting these enzymes can maintain the effectiveness of the natriuretic peptides.

Bristol Myers Squibb was the first company to test an active substance that was thought to inhibit both the ACE enzyme and neprilysin simultaneously. This was, however, never brought to market due to severe side-effects.

1

The combination of a neprilysin inhibitor (NI) with an angiotensin receptor blocker (ARB) eventually showed the desired effect – and with fewer side effects to boot. In 2003, Novartis patented LCZ696, a crystalline complex from two active substances, valsartan and sacubitril. Valsartan lowers blood pressure and sacubitril, or rather a metabolite of the substance, improves the flow of blood to the kidneys and water flow.

A further large-scale multinational study with 8,442 patients (PARADIGM-HF) in 2014 showed that LCZ696 reduced mortality and hospitalization by 20 per cent compared with enalapril, an established ACE inhibitor. The results of the study were convincing in the treatment of heart failure and highly promising.

From 2015, the first "angiotensin receptor neprilysin inhibitor" (ARNI) came on the market under the name of *Entresto*. The era of neuro-hormonal modulation was born.

A sticking point in these medicines is, however, precisely what makes them so effective, namely that they encroach into complex regulated body systems. *Entresto* thus still causes considerable side-effects. It leads to an imbalance in other metabolic systems, requiring additional medication to counteract. Additionally, *Entresto* is not recommended for patients who are diabetic or taking ACE inhibitors.

Heart failure develops gradually and unnoticed. This is because the body can compensate for the weakness of the heart at the beginning. As the weakness of the heart muscle is often not noticed until very late, its treatment is mostly only possible with medication. Heart failure can be prevented, however, through a healthy lifestyle supporting the drug therapy. This explains why the *Entresto* website also publishes healthy recipes and a recent 2020 study compares the effect of *Entresto* with a modified and healthier lifestyle.

There are also signs that, in the rich industrialized nations at least, blood pressure as a factor in cardiovascular problems had already subsided before special medicines like *Diovan* or *Entresto* came onto the market. In contrast to the 1960s, high blood pressure is not automatically a sign of affluence. It is regarded far more and in the first instance as a health problem connected to poverty, poor nutrition, unhealthy lifestyle and environmental factors such as air pollution.

On the other hand, cardiovascular problems remain high on the agenda for the ever ageing population, also of industrialized countries, even more so than cancer. In view of that situation, innovative solutions are in demand. With inclisiran, a "small interfering RNA" substance, Novartis is again at the starting point of the next innovation leap.

R137
Sacubitril Valsartan
Na Hydrate
(LCZ696/IP)

Reactor

Production

200- PG-13702

R137

GLEEVEC

From a gene defect to revolutionary leukemia treatment

In 1845, the Scottish physician John Bennett described the unusual case of a patient with a swelling on his spleen and whose physical condition rapidly worsened until he had tumors all over his body, suffered great pain and fever, and eventually died. As was customary at the time, he was treated with phlebotomies and enemas, which of course were no help. Bennett, however, observed that the patient's blood was full of white corpuscles. What was strange was that the doctor was unable to discover any source of infection even during the autopsy. He therefore assumed a kind of spontaneous "suppuration of the blood".

Some months later, Rudolph Virchow, later the founder of cellular pathology, called the blood of a female patient "white blood". He could not agree with the diagnosis of suppuration. Far more, he concluded that the observed white blood was caused by uninhibited, pathological division of the white corpuscles; this on the basis of two principles he had proposed, that living beings consist on the one hand of cells and on the other, that cells arise out of cells.

This thesis led to a fundamental paradigm shift in understanding cancer. For the first time, tumors were seen as rampant tissue and leukemia as cancer in liquid form. In time, different kinds of blood cancer were distinguished. Around 1900, it was known that the disease can occur acutely and aggressively as well as slowly, chronically and almost painlessly.

Chronic myeloid leukemia (CML) belongs to the latter category. It is mainly found in adults and can hardly be felt for years. At an advanced stage, however, it gives rise to fatigue, weight loss, enlargement of the spleen and eventually to the collapse of the immune system. If left untreated, patients rarely survive this final phase for more than a few months.

As opposed to solid tumors, there is no possibility of surgical removal for blood cancer, so for a long time treatment methods were limited. From 1920, the disease was treated with radiation. Between 1950 and 1960, various chemotherapies followed, but with massive side-effects and only a short extension of life. The only therapy with healing potential was, from the 1970s, bone marrow transplantation. With this, however, there is a great risk of an immune reaction against the transplanted bone marrow. Around a fifth of the patients die after the operation. Additionally, great age or other medical factors exclude transplantation in many cases.

From the later 1950s, scientists began to tackle the molecular and not least the genetic causes of cancer, and attempted to find commonalities between the various types. Researchers at the University of Pennsylvania in Philadelphia (USA) discovered in 1959 that chromosome 22 was shortened in all CML patients. This went down in history as the Philadelphia chromosome, after the place where it was discovered. It took another 14 years before other research groups found that the piece missing in chromosome 22 had attached itself to chromosome nine and vice versa. A mutual exchange of the chromosome parts, so to speak.

1
Sterile production system for *Gleevec* capsules. Stein site (Switzerland). June 2001.

2
Manufacturing *Gleevec* capsules. Stein site. June 2001.

In 1982, the two gene pieces were successfully sequenced, *Abl* on chromosome nine and *Bcr* on chromosome 22. The new piece on chromosome 22, the fusion product of the two gene pieces, was further investigated as *Bcr-Abl*, and confirmed in a 1987 animal study as the first human oncogene.

The *Bcr-Abl* gene in CML cells codes for a hyperactive enzyme which activates a signal path that in turn forces the cells to divide incessantly. The tyrosine kinase, as this enzyme is called, thus became the first target for a specific cancer treatment. It was now just a matter of finding a substance that, after the principle of lock and key, could react with the tyrosine kinase such that it would be inhibited without damaging healthy cells.

A research group at Ciba-Geigy immediately began to synthesize thousands of molecules that fit as closely as possible into the three-dimensional structure of tyrosine kinase and would thus inhibit it. At the beginning of the nineties, several molecules with the desired properties were available, among them a particularly promising one designated CGP57148. Initial tests with human CML cells in a university laboratory in Oregon (USA) were so successful that the clinical director there, Brian Druker, wanted to cement the cooperation with Ciba-Geigy and drive forward the development of a marketable medicine. At this time, however, the pharmaceutical industry in Basel was undergoing tremendous upheavals: it was the time of the merger between Ciba and Sandoz to form Novartis. New business models and new blockbusters were sought.

The high selectivity of the kinase inhibitor molecule was a scientific breakthrough, as for the first time it offered the possibility of a cancer therapy that hardly affected healthy cells in their function. Due to the limited indication, however, this selectivity represented a considerable economic risk. CML has a yearly incidence of around two new cases per 100,000 adults. This means a high development cost for the relatively few people that the drug would help. In the end, Novartis agreed to produce enough CGP57148 to allow a clinical study to be conducted. This study was a resounding success. Of the 54 patients in the first phase I study who received high doses of the medicine, 53 showed a full reaction within a few days.

As many of the first patients were still in full remission after a few months, the new medicine was classed as a clear success. In February 2001, barely 32 months after beginning the first clinical studies on humans, the Basel pharmaceutical company submitted applications for marketing licenses worldwide. The US authorities were the first to approve the product, in May 2001, under the trade name *Gleevec*. Since then, the success has continued; *Gleevec/Glivec* is still the standard therapy for CML today and registered for the treatment of certain forms of gastrointestinal stromal tumors as well. It is one of the few cancer drugs in tablet form, which makes the lifelong intake it requires relatively user-friendly. Even so, there have been setbacks with this specific therapy. Some patients develop resistance against *Gleevec* over time. This is a matter of a mutation which

1

2

specifically changes the structure of the resulting *Bcr-Abl* tyrosine kinase such that the active substance can no longer bind and so the uncontrolled division of the cancer cells starts again. New active substances with even stronger binding to the protein had to be developed. The successor product that Novartis brought to market, *Tasigna*, was first registered in Switzerland in 2007, and from 2010 as first therapy in Switzerland too.

So even with such a specific and effective medicine as *Gleevec*, the game of cat-and-mouse continues with cancer. Such challenges are not the smallest factor driving the pharmaceutical industry to make new improvements and innovations again and again. In constant life cycle management for every drug, both the active substances and the final products are optimized, including the manufacturing processes, supply chains and last but not least the costs.

COSENTYX

New hope against psoriasis

In ancient times, lepers were stigmatized and ostracized by society. Banished from settlements, they had to make themselves recognizable from far off, through bells, rattles and external features. This happened primarily because of society's helplessness faced with this strange disease, whose causes were seen as a punishment of god or an imbalance in bodily fluids, depending on the culture and epoch.

Until well into the 19th century, no clear distinction was made between leprosy, psora, leukoderma, lichen or pustules. Correspondingly, the therapies were undifferentiated too. For instance, according to the humorism theory, prominent at the time, attempts were made to drive out black bile from the body using purgatives, emetics or bleeding.

Only when microscopes became better and better, cells discovered, and bacteria isolated did the possibilities of diagnosis expand. At the same time, the descriptions of the appearance of skin diseases improved. At last, it became possible to differentiate more precisely. Between 1873 and 1880 the leprosy pathogen *Mycobacterium leprae* was discovered; leprosy was thus differentiated from eczema and psoriasis. For sufferers, perhaps the most important progress in diagnosis was the difference between "infectious" and "not infectious", which at least initiated their destigmatization. In contrast to leprosy, however, for which effective antibiotic therapies could later be developed, the treatment of psoriasis remained a challenge until the present day.

Really effective approaches to the treatment of the flaking, inflammatory skin abberations were far off. Quicksilver and arsenic ointments seemed to soothe the symptoms, but at the cost of severe side-effects. The first products of the pharmaceutical industry against psoriasis were ammonia, turpentine, tar or salicylic acid. Cortisone and vitamin D3 analogues followed. Light therapy, employed at first in sunlight sanatoria and later under artificial UV-B light sources, provided some relief as well. Despite initial pathophysiological explanations, however, hardly any better therapeutic possibilities emerged.

In the time after the Second World War, the components of blood and cells were analysed more and more precisely. This led to the discovery of the various peptides and antibodies. Depending on their amino acid sequence and three-dimensional structure, these play various roles in metabolism and immune defence. In 1957, interferon and its antiviral, immune-stimulating effect were discovered. In the 1960s, interleukins (neu-rotransmitters) were researched. As the name suggests, only their messenger function between white corpuscles was recognized at first. In the meantime, over 40 different interleukins are known. They interact in complex cascades between several types of cell and partly between themselves as well.

It was not until the 1980s that it became possible to manufacture these molecules on an industrial scale and thus employ them therapeutically. Although their structure was too complex to synthesize chemically,

1
Packaging labels for *Cosentyx*.
Stein site. March 2015.

the large target molecules were successfully obtained through fermentation, by genetically modifying bacteria or animal cells. In 1982, human insulin as the first biological was approved for the market. Many others followed. Above all the monoclonal antibodies, which permitted targeted intervention in the metabolism processes and immune responses, made possible the first therapies for previously incurable diseases.

Their production is, however, very complex and costly. The cells must first multiply in bioreactors, then the intermediate product be purified or modified in laborious, multi-step processes to make the final active substance. The final step is the formulation, mostly the sterile filling of syringes.

One of the interleukins, IL-17A, was identified as an important player in the inflammation processes of psoriasis. An antibody developed and biotechnologically manufactured by Novartis, named secukinumab, acts as an inhibitor of IL-17A. It is, however, used not only as a therapy for the affected areas of the skin, but also to cure the more severe cases of psoriatic arthritis, where the same factors lead to a rheumatic inflammation of the joints and even of some organs. In 2015, this medicine was approved for sale in the USA and Europe under the trade name *Cosentyx*. Clinical studies indicated significant superiority compared with other therapies. In 2020, approval was given for further indications in psoriasis.

The disease still cannot actually be cured, as its causes are inadequately understood even today. Nevertheless, *Cosentyx* has been able to improve the quality of life for more than 340,000 patients worldwide, who previously had little hope of relief.

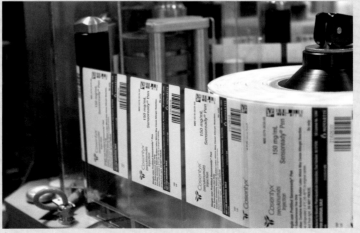

1

KYMRIAH AND ZOLGENSMA

Two game changers

Fifty years passed between James Watson's and Francis Crick's discovery of the double helix structure of DNA in 1953 and the decoding of the human genome in 2003. Since then, new approaches have been opening up in ever faster cycles to heal diseases that are either genetically conditioned or arise from mutations of DNA over the course of a lifetime.

Thanks to research into human metabolic, immunological or neurological systems, immune, cell and gene therapies could be developed to correct nature's mishaps.

When the modern pharmaceutical industry was in its infancy, natural substances were extracted and sometimes their molecular structure modified to make them more efficient or cause fewer side-effects. From the 1970s, biotechnological processes enabled the manufacture of larger molecules through to complex antibodies for which a chemical synthesis was too resource-intensive or indeed impossible with the means available. In this approach, microbes or animal cells are modified genetically such that they generate an active substance beneficial for humans in addition to their own metabolites. Cell and gene therapies now go a step further by genetically changing human cells *ex vivo* or *in vivo* directly to achieve the desired therapeutic effect.

The University of Pennsylvania in Philadelphia (USA) developed such a process to treat certain kinds of cancer. A type of white blood corpuscle, known as T-cells, plays an important part in the immune defence. The aim is to reprogram the T-cells genetically such that they are able not only to recognize cancer cells specifically, but also to bind and destroy them, i.e. the body's own immune system eliminates the diseased cells.

CAR-T is the umbrella term for therapies of this kind. It stands for chimeric antigen receptor T-cell, which means that the protein arising on the T-cell surface as chimera stimulates the immune response in a dual, reinforced way.

In 2012, Novartis and the University of Pennsylvania signed an exclusive contract to develop the CAR-T process further as CTL019 for various types of blood cancer, and make it ripe for the market.

This autologous process uses the patient's own cells and has the enormous advantage of obviating the need to spend months finding a suitable donor. That usually cannot be avoided in the case of bone marrow transplantation. Nevertheless, the success of the therapy depends greatly on the quality of the patient's cells.

In a special procedure, known as leucocyte apheresis, blood enriched with white corpuscles is taken from the patient. The cells then have to be transported as quickly as possible to the manufacturing plant. There, they are genetically modified and multiply, until they are finally harvested and formulated. After successful quality control, they are injected back into the patient via infusion. One of the first patients was Emily Whitehead in 2010. She was five years old, and her cancer had failed to respond to any of the therapies common at that time. The successful therapy and Emily's still

1
In a highly complex procedure, blood cells are suitably modified before being injected into the patient again. Novartis Morris Plains (New Jersey, USA). 2017.

2
An associate in cell and gene production prepares material for the actual production zone. Stein site (Canton of Aargau). 2019.

complete remission helped CTL019 to its breakthrough.

Already in May 2017, the FDA approved *Kymriah*, as the product is known commercially, in a fast-track procedure. Approval in Europe was gained the following year. In a first step, this procedure can be used in only two indications, leukemia and lymph gland cancer – and that only in patients suffering relapses after current treatment methods or who did not respond to them. How CAR-T therapy can tackle other types of cancer is now being researched.

To diversify in the field of gene therapy, Novartis took over the US company AveXis in 2018. As early as May 2019, *Zolgensma*, its top candidate to treat spinal muscular atrophy (SMA) in children under the age of two, was approved in the USA.

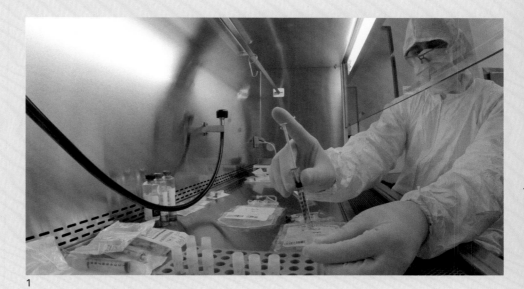

1

2

SMA results from a genetic defect. A gene known as SMN1 is essential for muscle building. If this is missing, not enough muscle cells can be formed. Vital functions like eating, breathing or mobility are so limited that the patient dies, usually just a few months after birth.

Whereas with *Kymriah* the patient's own T-cells are taken and reprogrammed, in the case of *Zolgensma* a synthetically manufactured SMN1 gene is injected. This intact SMN1 gene is only inserted into the patient's motor neuron cells, which multiply and thus produce the new gene themselves more and more. The patient's genetic material is not affected by this.

As well as the great hopes awakened by these new therapies for previously incurable illnesses, new economic and ethical questions have also arisen. Both products attracted the attention of the media, above all due to their uniquely high market prices of 475,000 US dollars for *Kymriah* and 2.1 million US dollars for *Zolgensma*.

Despite the great need, what has limited production capacities so far are the extremely difficult and mostly manually implemented procedures. A critical step in the manufacture is the implantation of the DNA. This employs viruses which have lost their pathogenic effects but which still have the capability of entering cells in a most effective way. Breeding these viruses is a slow process, resource-intensive and therefore costly.

The case of autologous therapies above all poses questions of role allocation, responsibility, and not least, property. Is the pharmaceutical manufacturer customer or supplier? Who is responsible if the production of a dose is unsuccessful? Do the modified T-cells belong exclusively to the patient? Are these "living medicines" really medicines, therapies, or indeed medical services? If the latter, can they be patented at all? In the case of the last chance of survival, should perhaps doses be made available to the patient which do not conform completely to the specifications of pharmaceutical legislation? And not least: how can such highly personalized therapies be assessed in accordance with the established guidelines for clinical studies?

In these first-in-class therapies, Novartis, together with the regional authorities, played a crucial part in developing new guidelines. Many questions are still unresolved, however, and must be posed for each and every new technique — from gene replacement therapy to genetic editing using CRISPR-Cas9, whose possibilities are now only being examined in early clinical trials, but whose principles were honored already in 2019 with the Nobel Prize for Chemistry.

If gene therapies can be shown to be more effective and safer than existing therapies, they will become the first-choice therapies of the future.

APPENDIX

Prix Galien

The Prix Galien was established in France in 1970. The aim of this new prize was to promote significant progress in pharmaceutical research. It is named after Galen, a physician of ancient Greece who is held to be one of the founding fathers of pharmacology. The prestigious reputation of the prize spread rapidly beyond the borders of France, with the consequence that many other countries set up their own Prix Galien. This explains why the same product can receive more than one award. The Prix Galien International has also existed since 1996, and is awarded every two years for the most important innovative developments. In scientific circles, the award is considered to be the "Nobel Prize for pharmacology".

The first ever Prix Galien was awarded in 1970 to CIBA for its antibiotic *Rimactane*. In 2002 and 2003, *Gleevec/Glivec* received the Prix Galien a total of ten times, including the Prix Galien International for therapeutic innovation (2002). Between 1970 and 2020, the Prix Galien was awarded to Novartis 61 times.

Year	Award-winning drugs	Origin	Number of Prix Galien awarded
1970	*Rimactane*	CIBA	1
1978	*Parlodel*	Sandoz	1
1984 | 1986 | 1992	*Sandimmune*	Sandoz	4
1991	*Sandostatin*	Sandoz	2
1999	*Simulect*	Novartis	1
2001	*Visudyne*	Novartis	2
2002	*Zometa*	Novartis	1
2002 | 2003	Gleevec/Glivec	Novartis	10
2006 | 2008	*Xolair*	Novartis	2
2008	*Exjade, Lucentis, Coartem*	Novartis	3
2011	*Ixiaro*	Novartis	1
2012	*Gilenya*	Novartis	2
2013	*Bexsero, Gilenya, Lucentis*	Novartis	3
2014	*Ilaris, Bexsero* (3), *Gilenya*	Novartis	5
2016	*Cosentyx* (2), *Entresto*	Novartis	3
2017	*Entresto* (2), *Gilenya* (2)	Novartis	4
2018	*Entresto* (2), *Kymriah*	Novartis	3
2019	*Kymriah* (7), *Rydapt, Luxturna* (3), *Kisqali*	Novartis	12
2020	*Aimovig*	Novartis	1

Sources and Bibliography

Archive records

Novartis Company Archive, Geigy record group
GL 1–27 | Management Committee minutes
VR 1, VR 1/1–1/11 | Board minutes

Novartis Company Archive, CIBA record group
Vg 1.01 | Management Committee minutes
Vg 1.02.1 | Internal Reports
VR 1 | Board Minutes

Novartis Company Archive, Sandoz record group
C-101.001 | Management reports and reports to the Board of Directors
C-102.001 | Board Minutes
C-304.001 | Management Minutes
C-311.001 | Chairman's Committee Minutes
H-433.001–015 | Pharmaceutical specialties: sales, statistics

Novartis Company Archive, Ciba-Geigy record group
KL 1 | Group Management Committee minutes
VR 1 | Board minutes

Published sources

J.R. Geigy A.G. Annual Report 1946–1969
Unsere Arbeit und wir or Geigy company newspaper 1943–1970
Statement of Account of the Gesellschaft für chemische Industrie in Basel 1885–1944
Statement of Account or Annual Report of CIBA AG 1945–1969
CIBA-Blätter 1943–1970
Report and Statement of Account of Chemische Fabrik vormals Sandoz 1912–1938
Report and Statement of Account of Sandoz AG 1939–1989
Sandoz AG Annual Report 1990–1995
Sandoz Bulletin 1965–1996
Ciba-Geigy AG Annual Report 1970–1991
Ciba Annual Report 1992
Ciba Abbreviated Report 1993–1995
Ciba-Geigy Zeitung or *Ciba Zeitung* 1970–1996
Novartis Business Overview 1996–2000
Financial Report of Novartis 1996–2000
Novartis Group Annual Report 2001–2017
Novartis Annual Report 2018–2020
Novartis Live 1996–2020

Bibliography

Author not named *Society of Chemical Industry in Basle, 1864–1926*. Basel 1928.

Bächi, Beat *LSD auf dem Land: Produktion und kollektive Wirkung psychotroper Stoffe.* Constance 2020.

Bürgi, Michael *Pharmaforschung im 20. Jahrhundert. Arbeit an der Grenze zwischen Hochschule und Industrie (Interferenzen – Studien zur Kulturgeschichte der Technik, Vol. 17).* Zurich 2011.

Bürgin, Alfred *Geschichte des Geigy-Unternehmens von 1758 bis 1939. Ein Beitrag zur Basler Unternehmer- und Wirtschaftsgeschichte.* Basel 1958.

Dettwiler, Walter *A Short History of the St. Johann Works*, in: *Novartis Campus: a Contemporary Work Environment Premises, Elements, Perspectives.* Ostfildern (Germany) 2009, pp. 44–55.

Fritz, Hans *Industrielle Arzneimittelherstellung. Die pharmazeutische Industrie in Basel am Beispiel der Sandoz AG (Heidelberger Schriften zur Pharmazie- und Naturwissenschaftsgeschichte, Vol. 10).* Stuttgart (Germany) 1992.

Janser, Andres / Junod, Barbara (Eds) *Corporate Diversity: Swiss Graphic Design and Advertising by Geigy 1940–1970.* Zurich 2009.

Klotzsche, Mario *Basler Farbenunternehmen und der synthetische Indigo. Die Grossprojekte von Ciba und Geigy vor dem Ersten Weltkrieg*, in: *Basler Zeitschrift für Geschichte und Altertumskunde*, Vol. 108 (2008), pp. 181–221.

Koelner, Paul *Aus der Frühzeit der chemischen Industrie Basels.* Basel 1937.

König, Mario *Besichtigung einer Weltindustrie – 1859 bis 2016 (Chemie und Pharma in Basel*, Vol. 1). Basel 2016.

Kreis, Georg et al. *Wechselwirkungen einer Beziehung – Aspekte und Materialien (Chemie und Pharma in Basel*, Vol. 2). Basel 2016.

Kutter, Markus (Ed.) *Geigy heute. Die jüngste Geschichte, der gegenwärtige Aufbau und die heutige Tätigkeit der J.R. Geigy A.G., Basel und der ihr nahestehenden Gesellschaften.* Basel 1958.

Meyer, Ulrich *Steckt eine Allergie dahinter? Die Industrialisierung von Arzneimittel-Entwicklung, -Herstellung und -Vermarktung am Beispiel der Antiallergika (Greifswalder Schriften zur Geschichte der Pharmazie und Sozialpharmazie, Vol. 4).* Stuttgart (Germany) 2002.

Moser, Patrick *Hohe Umsätze, tiefe Löhne? Die J. R. Geigy A.-G. und ihre Arbeiterschaft während des Ersten Weltkrieges*, in: *Basler Zeitschrift für Geschichte und Altertumskunde*, Vol. 114 (2014), pp. 115–141.

Ratmoko, Christina *Damit die Chemie stimmt. Die Anfänge der industriellen Herstellung von weiblichen und männlichen Sexualhormonen 1914–1938 (Interferenzen – Studien zur Kulturgeschichte der Technik*, Vol. 16). Zurich 2010.

Riedl, Renate A. *A Brief History of the Pharmaceutical Industry in Basel*, in: Higby, Gregory J./Stroud, Elaine C. (Eds): *Pill Peddlers: Essays on the History of the Pharmaceutical Industry.* Madison (USA) 1990, pp. 49–72.

Schröter, Harm G. *Unternehmensleitung und Auslandsproduktion: Entscheidungsprozesse, Probleme und Konsequenzen in der schweizerischen Chemieindustrie*, in: *Schweizerische Zeitschrift für Geschichte*, Vol. 44 No. 1 (1994), pp. 14–53.

Simon, Christian *Chemiestadt Basel*, in: Kreis, Georg / Wartburg, Beat von (Eds): *Basel – Geschichte einer städtischen Gesellschaft.* Basel 2000, pp. 364–383.

Straumann, Tobias *Die Schöpfung im Reagenzglas. Eine Geschichte der Basler Chemie (1850–1920).* Basel and Frankfurt am Main (Germany) 1995.

Straumann, Tobias *Farbstoffe gegen Rohstoffe: die Ciba und der Erste Weltkrieg*, in: Rossfeld, Roman / Straumann, Tobias (Eds): *Der vergessene Wirtschaftskrieg – Schweizer Unternehmen im Ersten Weltkrieg.* Zurich 2008, pp. 289–313.

Studer, Tobias *Diversification in the History of Sandoz*, in: *Sandoz Bulletin (Special Issue).* Basel 1986, pp. 16–46.

Tauber, Marianne *Farbmittel und ihre Handelsnamen (1860–1890). Auswirkungen auf Lithografie und Typografie*, in: Hassler, Uta (Ed.): *Polychromie & Wissen.* Munich 2019, pp. 190–223.

Zeller, Christian *Globalisierungsstrategien – der Weg von Novartis.* Berlin/Heidelberg (Germany) 2001.

Index

Photo credits

Most of the pictorial material is from the Novartis Company Archive.
Other photographs were supplied by: Museum für Gestaltung Zurich (graphics collection), Novartis Brand Service, Novartis Malaria Initiative, Novartis Public Relations Switzerland.

Angelus Com'l Studio, Portland (USA) page 67: top left
G. L. Arlaud, Lyon (France) page 65: top left
Arless Photographers, Dorval (Canada) page 139: top, second from left
Foto Ascher, Wörgl (Austria) page 139: top, first left
Photo Basilisk AG, Basel page 165: 100
Mitter Bedi Industrial Photographer, Mumbai (India) page 110: 061
W. A. Bernet, Sandoz Nuremberg (Germany) page 138: top
BM-Bild, Stockholm (Sweden) page 92: 052
Maurice Broomfield, London page 113: 065
Howard Brundrett, Basel page 160: 093; page 162: 095; page 165: top center and top right; page 175: 1
Fotografía Industrial Centelles, Barcelona (Spain) page 109: top center
Foto Comet, Zurich page 120: 077
Disdéri & Cie., Paris (André-Adolphe-Eugène Disdéri) page 20: 005
Atelier Eidenbenz, Basel page 63: top center; page 93: top center
Photo L'Épi, F. Devolder, Brussels (Belgium) page 65: top right
Fairchild Aerial Surveys Inc., New York page 91: 050
Christian Flierl, Basel page 165: top left
Photo Grignon, Chicago page 69: top center
René Groebli, Zurich page 123: top left and top center
Otto Gyssler, Geigy Basel page 115: top, second from left
Hamilton Studios, Mumbai (India) page 71: top right
Peter Heman, Basel page 112: top; page 113: top left
August Höflinger, Basel page 23: 009; page 24: 010
Jakob Höflinger, Basel page 19: 004
Carl Hoffmann, Basel page 71: top left
Theodor Carl Hoffmann, Basel page 51: top center and top right
Laurids Jensen/Novartis Live Magazine page 163: top right; page 187: 2
Kaufmann & Mory, Chicago page 69: 039
Carl Kling, Basel page 38: 015
Christian Küenzi, Kilchberg (Switzerland) page 139: top, first and second from right
Alexander Kumar/Novartis Foundation page169: 106
Mathias Leemann, Basel page 145: 089; page 147: 091 and 092; page 149: 1 and 2; page 161: 094; page 162: 096; page 163: top left; page 173: 4 and 5; page 179: 1 and 2
Leitner, Biochemie Kundl (Austria) page 115: 069
Ju. Mebius, Moscow (Russia) page 21: top right
Moeschlin + Baur, Basel page 123: top right
Pierre Moilliet, Geigy Basel page 99: 2
Novartis AG page 161: top right; page 165: top right; page 166: 102
Novartis Live Magazine page 168: top, second from left; page 169: top right; page 177: 2; page 183: 1; page 185: 1
Finbarr O'Connell, Cork (Ireland) page 144: 088
Mario Perotti, Milan (Italy) page 97: 058
William A. Roberts Film Co., Greensboro (USA) page 68: 038
Claire Roessiger, Basel page 69: top left; page 73: top; page 83: 4 and 5; page 94: 054
Umberto Romito © ZHdK, Zurich page 125: 1 to 3; page 127: 4 to 6
Armin Roth, Basel page 21: 006; page 36: 012 and 013; page 52: 025; page 53: 026; page 55: 1; page 62: 028; page 64: 031 and 032; page 68: 037; page 74: 044; page 79: 2 to 5; page 81: 1 and 2; page 92: 051; page 114: 066 to 068; page 118: 073; page 131: 8.2; page 142: 085; page 149: 3; page 164: 098; page 168: 104 and 105
Camille Ruf, Zurich page 50: 023
Antonio Santos d'Almeida, Lisbon (Portugal) page 118: 074
Schou-Jo, illustration og teknisk fotografi, Copenhagen (Denmark) page 111: top
Scott-d'Arazien, New York page 119: top center and top right
Josepho Shick, Shanghai (Anatol M. Josephewitz) page 77: 048 and top
Sives-Baffo, Milan (Italy) page 118: 075; page 119: 076
Robert Spreng, Basel page 93: top left
E. Stehle, Sandoz Basel page 72: 042; page 73: 043

Rémy Steinegger, Vaglio (Switzerland) page 169: top, second from left
Ezra Stoller, New York page 111: 062 and 063
Roland Tännler, Zurich page 167: top left
Tangram Partner, Basel page 169: top, second from right
Albert Teichmann, Basel page 63: top right; page 65: 033; page 70: 040; page 71: 041
Foto Trousil, Prague page 63: top left
Mark Tuschman, Menlo Park (USA)/Novartis Foundation page 99: 1 and page 101: 3
Alex Urosevic, Basel/Novartis AG page 166: 101
Laurence Voumard, Cologne (Germany) page 168: top
Roman Weyeneth, Basel page 164: 099
Fritz Wüthrich, CIBA Basel page 18: top; page 19: top
Guillermo Zamora, Mexico City page 108: 059 and top right
Harf Zimmermann, Berlin page 171: 2

Author

Walter Dettwiler has been Head of the Novartis Company Archive since 2004. He studied history and philosophy, and worked at the Swiss National Museum in Zurich and the Historical Museum in Basel. He was also active as a freelance historian. In addition to his publications, he has realized several exhibitions on wide-ranging historical themes.

With special thanks to
Matthias Leuenberger
Ursula Herz
Marcel Hugener
Thomas Hungerbühler
Peter Kornicker
Stephen Paul Lander
Barbara Luczak
Romeo Paioni (decd.)
Frank Petersen
Michael Plüss
Wolfdietrich Schutz
Florence Wicker

First published in this English-language translation in 2021 by
Profile Books Ltd
29 Cloth Fair
London
EC1A 7JQ
www.profilebooks.com

Newly revised, extended and enhanced edition of the book
Novartis – How a leader in healthcare was created out of Ciba, Geigy and Sandoz
(ISBN 978 1 78125 265 9)
published by Profile Books in 2014

ISBN 978 1 78816 981 3

Design Focus Grafik, Karin Rütsche, Basel, Switzerland
Repro Bildpunkt AG, Münchenstein, Switzerland
Printed by Gremper AG, Basel, Switzerland
Bound by Bubu AG, Mönchaltorf, Switzerland